# CONTENTS

Carla Bardi

# Spaghetti

BARRON'S

# INTRODUCTION

# Introduction

Without doubt, spaghetti is the most popular and best known pasta shape in the world, symbol of all things Italian. Yet spaghetti was the last among the classic shapes to appear on the crowded Italian pasta scene. It was invented in the beautiful southern city of Naples. The word first appears in a short poem written by Antonio Viviani in 1824, entitled, not surprisingly, *Macaroni in Naples*.

Long and cylindrical in shape, spaghetti was originally thinner, more like modern spaghettini or vermicelli. Later, when served with richer northern sauces, it needed to be thicker and consequently became the fatter spaghetti we know today.

In this book we feature dozens of recipes for serving spaghetti, but we have also chosen sauces for thin spaghettini, flattened linguine (also known as bavette and trenette), bucatini (with a hole in the center), and thick ziti. These recipes reflect the traditional Italian way of serving spaghetti, which lightly dresses the pasta without over-whelming it. If you prefer spaghetti with a lot of sauce, increase the liquid measurements accordingly.

## Cooking Tips

**Timing:** One of the most difficult things for the novice pasta cook is knowing when the pasta is ready. It should be boiled until the outer layers are soft enough to absorb the delicious sauce you have prepared, while the inside is

p. 50

Here you will find more than 130 mouthwatering recipes for spaghetti and other types of long pasta. Buon appetito!

p. 212

p. 148

p. 182

firm enough to pose some resistance to the bite. This is called "al dente."

**Water:** Pasta needs lots of water to cook properly. Allow about 4 quarts (4 liters) for each pound (500 g) of pasta. Never cook even a small amount of pasta in less than 3 quarts (3 liters).

**Salt:** Allow at least 1 heaped tablespoon of salt for each pound (500 g) of pasta. Add the salt once the water is boiling, just before adding the pasta.

**Quantity:** As a general guideline, allow about 4 ounces (125 g) per head. If the pasta is a first course between an appetizer and the main course, you may need less. If you are just serving pasta with a salad, you may need more.

**Cooking:** When the water is boiling, add all the pasta at once. Stir with a wooden spoon so it doesn't stick together. Cover the pot with a lid and bring it back to a boil as soon as possible. When the water is boiling again, leave to cook uncovered, stirring often.

**Draining:** Drain the pasta in a colander as soon as it is cooked. Don't leave it sitting in the water or it will become overcooked.

**Serving:** Pasta should be served immediately. If it is left sitting, it will turn into a sticky lump.

Last but not least, always remember that the wonderful thing about Italian food is that you can invent and improvise according to your mood and what you have in the refrigerator. Use these recipes as a basis, then branch out on your own. The important thing is to enjoy—both the cooking and the eating!

# Types of
# Spaghetti

Angel's hair

# Spaghettini

# Spaghetti

# Bucatini

Linguine

Ziti

Spaghetti is now made in a variety of colors and flavors, including spinach, whole-wheat (wholemeal), tomato, chile, nettle, and many more. Care should be taken in matching the flavors of these spaghetti types with sauces so that they don't clash. Traditional spaghetti is a vehicle for the sauce, whereas these new types have their own personalities which must be taken into consideration.

Tomato spaghetti

Cook the spaghetti in a large pot of salted boiling water until al dente.

While the pasta is cooking, chop the basil, garlic, walnuts, and pine nuts in a food processor. Gradually add the oil as you chop.

Transfer the pesto to a small bowl. Stir in the cheese and season with salt and pepper.

Drain the pasta and place in a heated serving bowl. Add the pesto and toss gently. Garnish with the extra basil and serve hot.

# Spaghettini
# **with garlic, mint & olives**

| | |
|---|---|
| $1/3$ | cup (90 ml) extra-virgin olive oil |
| 2 | cloves garlic, finely chopped |
| 6 | anchovy fillets |
| 2 | tablespoons finely chopped fresh mint |
| 4 | tablespoons finely chopped fresh parsley |
| 1 | pound (500 g) spaghetti |
| 2 | tablespoons salt-cured capers, rinsed |
| 12 | large black olives, pitted and coarsely chopped |

# Whole-wheat spaghetti

p. 70

Enjoy the pungent flavors of fresh herbs or savor the naturally sweet taste of fruit in these sauces.

p. 32

p. 64

p. 28

p. 46

# FRESH HERBS, FLOWERS & FRUIT

p. 42

p. 48

p. 54

# Fresh herbs, flowers & fruit

**Basil:** Pungent, fresh basil is the key ingredient in pesto and many other pasta sauces. Buy it fresh, or cultivate it in a window box (it's very easy to grow).

**Chile:** Also known as chilli, chili, and chile pepper. Spicy chilies originally come from Central America but have spread to cuisines around the world. Fresh or dried chile is usually better than the powdered variety (which ages rapidly after crushing).

**Flowers:** Not all flowers are edible, but sunflowers and roses not only taste good but look very pretty when used as a garnish. Be sure that any flower to be eaten has not been sprayed with pesticides.

**Garlic:** Spicy when eaten raw and mellow when cooked, garlic is an essential ingredient in a host of pasta sauces. It is also very good for your health, and many believe it lowers cholesterol and blood pressure, as well as fighting off cancer.

**Lemon:** Full of vitamin C and with a refreshing tarty taste, freshly squeezed lemon juice can be used to prevent apples, pears, artichokes, and other ingredients from turning brown. Small quantities of fresh zest and juice added to pasta sauces will highlight other flavors.

**Marjoram:** With its delicate pine and lemon scents, marjoram is a perfect addition to many types of pasta sauces.

**Melon:** Cube a sweet cantaloupe (rock melon)

and heat it with garlic and cream for a healthy summertime pasta sauce.

**Mint:** Strongly scented and aromatic, mint makes a great addition to pasta salads, but is also good with many hot pasta sauces.

**Nuts:** Pine nuts, walnuts, pistachios, and hazelnuts can be toasted and added to pasta dishes as a tasty garnish.

**Oranges:** Fresh, in-season slices of orange make a healthful addition to pasta sauces based on tomato. Or serve with pasta by themselves, along with fresh creamy cheese, garlic, oil, and finely chopped fresh herbs.

**Parsley:** Curly leaf or flat leaf (Italian) parsley are used to flavor and garnish many pasta sauces. Always buy parsley fresh and chop just before use.

**Pesto:** The word comes from the Italian verb "pestare," meaning to crush. The original pesto, from Liguria, was made from basil, pine nuts, garlic, and oil. Nowadays many different types of pesto are made—try our marjoram pesto on page 48.

**Rosemary:** Originating in the Mediterranean, rosemary is widely used in Italian cuisine. A sprig or two can be added to flavor a sauce, or the tiny needles can be finely chopped and added. Fresh rosemary has a strong flavor—take care not to add too much or it will overpower other flavors.

**Sage:** Fresh sage has a strong flavor that melds beautifully with butter to flavor an array of pasta dishes.

# Spaghetti
# **with nutty pesto**

| | |
|---|---|
| 1 | pound (500 g) spaghetti |
| 1 | large bunch fresh basil leaves + extra leaves, to garnish |
| 2 | cloves garlic |
| 20 | walnuts, shelled |
| 4 | tablespoons pine nuts |
| 1/2 | cup (125 ml) extra-virgin olive oil |
| 1/2 | cup (60 g) freshly grated pecorino cheese |
| | Salt and freshly ground black pepper |

Heat the oil in a large frying pan over medium heat. Add the garlic and sauté until pale gold, 2–3 minutes.

Add the anchovies and simmer—crushing with a wooden spoon—until they have dissolved into the oil, about 5 minutes.

Remove from the heat and add the mint and parsley.

Meanwhile, cook the pasta in a large pot of salted boiling water until al dente.

Drain the pasta and add to the sauce. Sprinkle with the capers and olives, toss well, and serve hot.

# Spaghetti
# with lemon,
# black olives
# & basil

| | |
|---|---|
| 1 | pound (500 g) spaghetti |
| 1/2 | cup (125 ml) extra-virgin olive oil |
| | Zest of 2 lemons, cut into julienne strips |
| | Freshly squeezed juice of 2 lemons |
| 1 1/2 | cups (150 g) pitted black olives, coarsely chopped |
| 2 | cloves garlic, finely chopped |
| 15 | small fresh basil leaves |
| | Salt and freshly ground black pepper |

Cook the spaghetti in a large pot of salted boiling water until al dente.

While the pasta is cooking, beat together the oil, lemon zest, lemon juice, black olives, garlic, and basil in a large bowl. Season with salt and pepper.

Drain the pasta and add to the bowl with the sauce. Toss well and serve hot.

# Spaghetti
# **with tomato, lemon & basil**

| | |
|---|---|
| 1 | pound (500 g) spaghetti |
| 2 | pounds (1 kg) ripe tomatoes |
| | Small bunch fresh basil leaves |
| $1/3$ | cup (90 ml) extra-virgin olive oil |
| | Freshly squeezed juice of 1 lemon |
| 2 | cloves garlic, finely chopped |
| | Salt and freshly ground black pepper |

Cook the spaghetti in a large pot of salted boiling water until al dente.

While the pasta is cooking, blanch the tomatoes in boiling water for 2 minutes. Drain and slip off the skins. Chop coarsely.

Drain the pasta and transfer to a large serving bowl.

Add the tomatoes, basil, oil, lemon juice, and garlic. Season with salt and pepper. Toss well and serve hot.

# Spaghetti
# **with chile oil**

Chile Oil

4–6 small, dried chilies

| | |
|---|---|
| 1 | cup (250 ml) extra-virgin olive oil |

| | |
|---|---|
| 1 | pound (500 g) spaghetti |
| 3 | cloves garlic, lightly crushed but whole |
| 1/2 | cup (75 g) fine dry bread crumbs |

Chile Oil: Crumble the chilies into a small glass jar or bowl. Add the oil and stir gently. Allow to steep for several hours. Sealed in an airtight container the oil will keep for several weeks. It can be served with pasta, boiled rice or vegetables, pizza, or fish.

Cook the spaghetti in a large pot of salted boiling water until al dente.

While the pasta is cooking, heat 2 tablespoons of the chile oil in a large frying pan over medium heat. Add the garlic and sauté until pale gold, 2–3 minutes.

Drain the pasta and add to the pan. Add chile oil to taste and the bread crumbs. Toss gently and serve hot.

# Spaghetti
# **with arugula, chile & garlic**

| | |
|---|---|
| 1 | pound (500 g) spaghetti |
| 1 | large bunch arugula (rocket) |
| $1/3$ | cup (90 ml) extra-virgin olive oil |
| 4 | cloves garlic, finely chopped |
| 1–2 | small dried chilies, crumbled |
| 4–6 | anchovy fillets (optional) |
| | Salt |

Cook the spaghetti in a large pot of salted boiling water for 10 minutes.

Add the arugula and continue cooking until the pasta is al dente, 1–2 minutes.

While the pasta is cooking, heat the oil in a large frying pan over medium heat. Add the garlic, chilies, and anchovies, if using, and sauté for 2–3 minutes. Do not let the garlic burn.

Drain the pasta and arugula and add to the pan with the garlic and oil. Season with salt. Toss gently and serve hot.

# Spaghettini
# **with brandy**
# **& herbs**

| | |
|---|---|
| 1/4 | cup (60 ml) extra-virgin olive oil |
| 1 | onion, finely chopped |
| 2 | cloves garlic, finely chopped |
| 1 | tablespoon finely chopped fresh sage |
| 1 | tablespoon finely chopped fresh rosemary |
| 1 | tablespoon finely chopped fresh mint |
| 2 | tablespoons finely chopped fresh parsley |
| 5 | tablespoons brandy |
| 1 | pound (500 g) spaghettini |
| | Salt and freshly ground black pepper |
| 1 | cup (125 g) freshly grated Parmesan cheese |

Heat the oil in a large frying pan over medium heat. Add the onion and garlic and sauté for 2 minutes. Add the herbs and sauté for 2–3 minutes.

Pour in the brandy and simmer for 2–3 minutes.

Meanwhile, cook the pasta in a large pot of salted boiling water until al dente.

Drain well and place in the pan with the sauce. Season with salt and pepper and sprinkle with the cheese. Toss well and serve hot.

# Linguine
# **with garlic**
# **& anchovies**

| | |
|---|---|
| 1 | pound (500 g) linguine |
| 1/3 | cup (90 ml) extra-virgin olive oil |
| 8 | salt-cured anchovy fillets, finely chopped |
| 8 | cloves garlic, finely chopped |
| 4 | tablespoons finely chopped fresh parsley |
| 1 | small dried chile, crumbled |

Cook the pasta in a large pot of salted boiling water until al dente.

While the pasta is cooking, heat the oil in a large frying pan over medium heat. Add the anchovies and stir with a wooden spoon until they dissolve in the oil.

Add the garlic, parsley, and chile and simmer for 1 minute.

Drain the pasta and add to the pan. Toss well and serve hot.

# Spaghetti
## with melon, cream & parmesan

| | |
|---|---|
| 1 | pound (500 g) spaghetti |
| 1 | tablespoon extra-virgin olive oil |
| 1 | small clove garlic, very finely chopped |
| 1 | cup (250 g) heavy (double) cream |
| 1/2 | cup (125 ml) dry Marsala wine |
| 1 | small ripe cantaloupe (rock melon), peeled and cut in small cubes |
| | Salt and freshly ground black pepper |
| 6 | tablespoons freshly grated Parmesan cheese |

First English language edition for the United States and Canada published in 2010 by Barron's Educational Series, Inc.

© 2009 McRae Books Srl

This book was created and produced by McRae Books

Via del Salviatino, 1
50016 Fiesole - Florence Italy
info@mcraebooks.com
wwwmcraebooks.com
Publishers: Anne McRae, Marco Nardi

*Project Director* Anne McRae

*Art Director* Marco Nardi

*Photography* Brent Parker Jones
    R&RPHOTOSTUDIO

*Text* Carla Bardi

*Editing* Rosanne Johnson

*Food Styling* Michelle Finn

*Food styling assistants*
    Sebastian Sedlak,
    Giuliano Panetta

*Layouts* Aurora Granata

*Prepress* Filippo Delle Monache,
    Davide Gasparri

*All inquiries should be addressed to:*

Barron's Educational Series, Inc.

250 Wireless Boulevard

Hauppauge, New York 11788

www.barronseduc.com

ISBN-13: 978-0-7641-6308-1

ISBN-10: 0-7641-6308-6

*Library of Congress Control
    Number:* 2009928710

NOTE TO OUR READERS
Eating eggs that are not completely cooked poses the possibility of salmonella food poisoning. The risk is greater for pregnant women, the elderly, the very young, and persons with impaired immune systems. If you are concerned about salmonella, use reconstituted powdered egg whites or pasteurized eggs.

Printed in China
9 8 7 6 5 4 3 2 1

Cook the pasta in a large pot of salted boiling water until al dente.

While the pasta is cooking, heat the oil in a large frying pan over medium heat. Add the garlic and sauté until pale gold, 2–3 minutes.

Pour in the cream and Marsala and add the melon. Simmer for 4–5 minutes. Season with salt and pepper.

Drain the pasta, toss with the sauce, and place in a heated serving dish. Sprinkle with the cheese, toss well, and serve hot.

# Spaghetti
# **with yogurt & avocado**

| | |
|---|---|
| 1 | ripe avocado, peeled, pitted, and diced |
| | Freshly squeezed juice of 1 lemon |
| 1 | pound (500 g) spaghetti |
| 1/4 | cup (60 ml) extra-virgin olive oil |
| 2 | cloves garlic, finely chopped |
| 1 | large onion, chopped |
| 1 | tablespoon dry white wine |
| 1 | cup (250 ml) plain yogurt |
| | Salt and freshly ground black pepper |
| 1 | fresh red chile, thinly sliced |
| 1 | celery heart, thinly sliced |
| 2 | tablespoons salt-cured capers, rinsed |
| 1 | tablespoon finely chopped fresh parsley |

Drizzle the avocado with the lemon juice to prevent it from browning.

Cook the pasta in a large pot of salted boiling water until al dente.

While the pasta is cooking, heat the 2 tablespoons of oil in a large frying pan over medium heat. Sauté the garlic and onion until pale gold, 2–3 minutes. Add the wine and simmer until evaporated.

Beat the yogurt with the remaining 2 tablespoons of oil in a large bowl. Season with salt and pepper. Add the chile, celery, capers, and parsley.

Drain the pasta and add to the bowl with the yogurt sauce. Add the onion mixture and avocado. Toss well and serve hot.

# Spaghetti
# **with red rose & sunflower petals**

| | |
|---|---|
| 1/4 | cup (60 ml) extra-virgin olive oil |
| 2 | cloves garlic, finely chopped |
| 1 | (14-ounce/400-g) can tomatoes, with juice |
| | Petals from 1 sunflower, coarsely chopped (leave a few whole, to garnish) |
| | Petals from 1 red rose, coarsely chopped (leave a few whole, to garnish) |
| 1 | small bunch basil, torn + extra leaves, to garnish |
| | Salt and freshly ground black pepper |
| 1/4 | cup (60 ml) dry white wine |
| 1 | pound (500 g) spaghetti |
| 1/2 | cup (60 g) freshly grated Parmesan cheese |

Heat the oil in a large frying pan over medium heat. Add the garlic and sauté until pale gold, 2–3 minutes.

Add the tomatoes, chopped sunflower and rose petals, and basil. Season with salt and pepper. Simmer for 15 minutes, adding the wine as the sauce reduces.

Cook the pasta in a large pot of salted boiling water until al dente.

Drain and add to the pan with the sauce. Sprinkle with the Parmesan and garnish with the basil and the reserved flower petals. Toss gently and serve hot.

# Linguine
# **with marjoram pesto**

| | |
|---|---|
| 1 | pound (500 g) linguine |
| 2 | cloves garlic |
| 1/4 | cup (45 g) pine nuts |
| | Salt |
| 1/2 | cup (125 ml) extra-virgin olive oil |
| | Large bunch fresh marjoram |
| 1/2 | cup (60 g) freshly grated Parmesan cheese |

Cook the pasta in a large pot of salted boiling water until al dente.

While the pasta is cooking, chop the garlic, pine nuts, salt, marjoram, and half the oil in a food processor until smooth. Stir in the Parmesan and a little more of the oil. Mix well.

Drain the pasta, reserving 2 tablespoons of the cooking water.

Place in a large bowl and add the pesto, reserved cooking water, and remaining oil. Toss well and serve hot.

# Spaghetti
## with garlic, pine nuts & raisins

| | |
|---|---|
| 1 | pound (500 g) spaghetti |
| $1/3$ | cup (90 ml) extra-virgin olive oil |
| 2 | cloves garlic, finely chopped |
| 1 | fresh red chile, seeded and finely chopped |
| $1/2$ | cup (90 g) pine nuts |
| $1/2$ | cup (90 g) golden raisins (sultanas) |
| | Salt and freshly ground black pepper |
| 4 | tablespoons finely chopped fresh parsley |

Cook the pasta in a large pot of salted boiling water until al dente.

Heat the oil in a large frying pan over medium heat. Add the garlic and chile and sauté until the garlic turns pale gold, 2–3 minutes.

Add the pine nuts and golden raisins. Season with salt and pepper. Sauté for 1 minute more.

Drain the pasta and add to the pan with the sauce. Add the parsley and toss over high heat. Serve hot.

# Spaghetti
# **with herbs**

| | |
|---|---|
| 1 | large bunch fresh basil |
| 1 | tablespoon finely chopped fresh rosemary |
| 2 | tablespoons finely chopped fresh parsley |
| 4 | tablespoons fine dry bread crumbs |
| 1/2 | cup (125 ml) extra-virgin olive oil |
| 2 | scallions (spring onions), finely sliced |
| 1 | clove garlic, finely chopped |
| 1 | tablespoon salt-cured capers, rinsed |
| 1 | cup (100 g) black olives, pitted and chopped |
| 1 | pound (500 g) spaghetti |
| | Freshly ground black pepper |

Chop the basil coarsely, reserving 16 large leaves. Mix the chopped basil, rosemary, parsley, and bread crumbs in a bowl.

Heat 3 tablespoons of oil in a large frying pan over medium heat. Add the scallions, garlic, capers, and olives and sauté for 3 minutes. Add the chopped herb mixture and sauté for 2 more minutes.

Sauté the reserved basil leaves in 3 tablespoons of oil in a small frying pan over medium heat for a few seconds, or until wilted. Drain on paper towels.

Cook the pasta in a large pot of salted boiling water until al dente.

Drain and add to the pan with the scallions and herbs. Sauté for 1 minute over medium heat. Season with pepper. Drizzle with the remaining oil and top with the basil. Serve hot.

# Spaghetti
# **with Sicilian pesto**

| | |
|---|---|
| 4 | large ripe tomatoes, peeled and chopped |
| 3 | tablespoons salt-cured capers, rinsed |
| 4 | tablespoons almonds |
| 3 | sprigs fresh parsley |
| 1 | sprig fresh mint |
| 1 | sprig fresh basil + extra leaves, to garnish |
| 2 | cloves garlic, peeled |
| 1/2 | fresh red chile, seeded and finely chopped |
| 1/3 | cup (90 ml) extra-virgin olive oil |
| | Salt |
| 1 | pound (500 g) cherry tomatoes, cut in half |
| 1 | pound (500 g) spaghetti |
| 12 | caperberries (cocktail capers) |

Place the chopped tomatoes, capers, almonds, parsley, mint, basil, 1 clove of garlic, chile, and ¼ cup (60 ml) of oil in a food processor and chop until smooth. Season with salt.

Slice the remaining garlic. Heat the remaining oil in a large frying pan over medium heat. Add the garlic and cherry tomatoes and sauté until the tomatoes have softened, about 5 minutes.

Cook the pasta in a large pot of salted boiling water until al dente.

Drain and add to the pan with the tomatoes. Add the pesto and toss well. Garnish with the extra basil and caperberries. Serve hot.

# Spaghetti
# **with kiwi fruit**

| | |
|---|---|
| 1 | pound (500 g) spaghetti |
| 4 | kiwi fruit |
| 1 | cup (250 ml) thick creamy plain (Greek-style) yogurt |
| 2 | cloves garlic, finely chopped |
| 1 | tablespoon finely grated lemon zest |
| | Salt and freshly ground black pepper |

Cook the pasta in a large pot of salted boiling water until al dente.

While the pasta is cooking, peel the kiwi fruit and chop two coarsely. Mash the remaining ones with a fork.

Warm the yogurt in a small saucepan over medium heat. Add the garlic, chopped kiwi fruit, and lemon zest. Season with salt and pepper. Simmer for 2–3 minutes, stirring constantly. Remove from the heat and add the mashed kiwis.

Drain the pasta and place in a large serving bowl. Add the sauce. Toss well and serve hot.

# Spaghetti
## with olive pesto & fried tomatoes

| | |
|---|---|
| 14 | ounces (400 g) firm-ripe tomatoes |
| 1 | small bunch fresh parsley |
| 1 | cup (100 g) green olives, pitted |
| 6 | tablespoons pine nuts |
| 1 | tablespoon sea salt |
| 6 | tablespoons freshly grated Parmesan cheese |
| 1/3 | cup (90 ml) extra-virgin olive oil |
| 1/2 | cup (125 ml) olive oil, for frying |
| 1/2 | cup (75 g) all-purpose (plain) flour |
| | Salt |
| 1 | pound (500 g) spaghetti |

Peel the tomatoes and slice thinly. Drain on paper towels. Set aside in the refrigerator, changing the paper a couple of times, to drain as much as possible.

Chop the parsley, olives, pine nuts, and sea salt in a food processor until smooth. Add the Parmesan. Gradually stir in the extra-virgin olive oil.

Heat the frying oil in a large frying pan until very hot. Dip the tomato slices in flour until well coated. Fry in small batches until crisp. Drain on paper towels. Sprinkle with salt.

Cook the pasta in a large pot of salted boiling water until al dente.

Drain into a serving bowl and toss with the olive pesto. Top with the fried tomatoes. Serve hot.

# Whole-wheat spaghetti **with walnuts & watercress**

| | |
|---|---|
| 1 | pound (500 g) whole-wheat (wholemeal) spaghetti |
| 1 | tablespoon extra-virgin olive oil |
| 1 | onion, finely chopped |
| 2 | cloves garlic, finely chopped |
| 2 | ounces (60 g) button mushrooms, sliced |
| 1 | cup (150 g) coarsely chopped walnuts |
| 1 | large bunch fresh watercress |
| 1 | cup (250 ml) sour cream |
| | Salt and freshly ground black pepper |

Cook the spaghetti in a large pot of salted boiling water until al dente.

While the pasta is cooking, heat the oil in a large frying pan over medium heat. Add the onion and garlic and sauté until pale gold, 2–3 minutes. Add the mushrooms and walnuts and simmer for 2–3 minutes.

Remove from the heat. Stir in the watercress and sour cream. Season with salt and pepper. Reheat over very low heat—do not allow the sauce to boil.

Drain the pasta into a serving bowl. Pour the sauce over the top and serve hot.

# Spaghetti
# **with scallions & herbs**

| 7 | tablespoons extra-virgin olive oil |
|---|---|
| 1¹/₂ | pounds (750 g) scallions (spring onions), sliced |
| 3 | doves garlic, finely chopped |
| 1 | bouquet garni |
| 8 | ounces (250 g) ripe tomatoes, peeled and chopped |
| 2 | fresh red chilies, sliced |
| 1 | pound (500 g) spaghetti |
|  | Fresh basil leaves |
|  | Salt |

Heat the oil in a large frying pan over low heat. Add the scallions, garlic, and bouquet garni and

sweat, uncovered, stirring frequently, until soft and reduced to less than a quarter of their original volume, about 20 minutes. Discard the bouquet garni.

Add the tomatoes and chilies to the pan with the scallions. Season with salt and simmer for 5 minutes, stirring occasionally. Remove from the heat.

Cook the spaghetti in a large pot of salted boiling water until al dente. Drain, reserving 3 tablespoons of the cooking water.

Add the spaghetti and cooking water to the pan with the scallions. Toss gently. Drizzle with the remaining oil and garnish with the basil. Serve hot.

# Spaghetti
# **with butter & pine nuts**

| | |
|---|---|
| 1 | pound (500 g) spaghetti |
| 1/2 | cup (125 g) best quality salted butter |
| 1/2 | cup (100 g) pine nuts |
| 2 | tablespoons finely chopped fresh parsley |
| | Coarsely ground black pepper |
| | Freshly grated Parmesan cheese |

Cook the spaghetti in a large pot of salted boiling water until al dente.

While the pasta is cooking, cook the butter in a large frying pan over medium-low high heat until the foam turns slightly brown and subsides. Set aside.

Toast the pine nuts in a heavy saucepan over medium heat, 3-4 minutes, shaking the pan often.

Drain the pasta and place in a large bowl. Drizzle with the butter. Add the pine nuts and parsley and season generously with pepper. Top with the Parmesan and serve hot.

# Spaghetti
# **with garlic, chile & oil**

| | |
|---|---|
| 1 | pound (500 g) spaghetti |
| 1/2 | cup (125 ml) extra-virgin olive oil |
| 8 | cloves garlic, finely chopped |
| 3 | small dried chilies, crumbled |
| 4 | tablespoons finely chopped fresh parsley |

Cook the spaghetti in a large pot of salted boiling water until al dente.

While the pasta is cooking, heat the oil in a large frying pan over medium heat. Sauté the chile and garlic until the garlic is pale gold, 2–3 minutes.

Drain the pasta and add to the frying pan. Sprinkle with the parsley and toss over medium heat for 1–2 minutes. Serve hot.

# Spaghetti
## with olives, anchovies & walnuts

| | |
|---|---|
| 1 | pound (500 g) spaghetti |
| $1/3$ | cup (90 ml) extra-virgin olive oil |
| 8 | salt-cured anchovy fillets |
| 1 | cup (100 g) pitted black olives, sliced |
| 20 | walnuts, halved |
| | Coarsely chopped fresh parsley |

Cook the spaghetti in a large pot of salted boiling water until al dente.

While the pasta is cooking, heat the oil in a large frying pan over medium heat. Add the anchovies and olives and stir with a wooden spoon until the anchovies dissolve.

Toast the walnuts in a small frying pan over medium heat, 3–4 minutes.

Drain the pasta and add to the pan with the anchovies. Add the walnuts and parsley. Toss well and serve hot.

# Homemade spaghetti **with garlic & oil**

Pasta Dough

2¹⁄₃ cups (350 g) all-purpose (plain) flour

¹⁄₄ teaspoon salt

Lukewarm water

¹⁄₂ cup (125 ml) extra-virgin olive oil

6 cloves garlic, finely chopped

6 tablespoons finely chopped fresh parsley

Sift the flour and salt into a mound on a work surface and make a well in the center. Add enough water to make a stiff dough. Knead for 15–20 minutes. Set aside for 30 minutes.

Break off pieces of dough and roll them into 8-inch (20-cm) long spaghetti. Use flour to prevent sticking. Leave the spaghetti to dry on the board covered with a cloth for at least 1 hour.

Cook the pasta in a large pot of salted boiling water until al dente. Drain and transfer to serving plates.

Heat the oil with the garlic in a small saucepan over medium heat until the garlic is pale gold, 2–3 minutes. Add to the pasta along with the parsley. Toss well and serve hot.

# Spaghetti
# **with sundried tomatoes**

| 1 | pound (500 g) spaghetti |
|---|---|
| 8 | ounces (250 g) sundried tomatoes packed in oil, finely sliced |
| 1 | small dried chile, crumbled |
| | Salt and freshly ground black pepper |
| | Fresh basil leaves |
| 1/2 | cup (60 g) shaved caciocavallo or provolone cheese |

Cook the pasta in a large pot of salted boiling water until al dente.

While the pasta is cooking, pour the oil from the sun-dried tomatoes, about ½ cup (125 ml), into a frying pan. Heat over medium heat then add the tomatoes. Sauté briefly then season with the chile, salt, and pepper.

Drain the pasta and add to the pan with the tomatoes. Sprinkle with the basil. Top with the cheese and serve hot.

# Spaghetti
## with oranges

| | |
|---|---|
| 1 | pound (500 g) spaghetti |
| 1/3 | cup (90 ml) extra-virgin olive oil |
| 2 | cloves garlic, finely chopped |
| 8 | anchovy fillets |
| 2 | tablespoons fine dry bread crumbs |
| 1/4 | cup (60 ml) dry white wine |
| 3 | oranges, peeled and cut into segments |
| | Salt |
| 1 | tablespoon finely chopped fresh parsley |

Cook the pasta in a large pot of salted boiling water until al dente.

While the pasta is cooking, heat the oil in a large frying pan over medium heat. Add the garlic and anchovies. Stir with a wooden spoon until the anchovies dissolve.

Add the bread crumbs and cook 2–3 minutes. Pour in the wine and simmer until evaporated.

Add the oranges and their juice. Simmer for 2 minutes. Season with salt.

Drain the pasta and place in a heated serving dish. Add the sauce and parsley. Toss gently and serve hot.

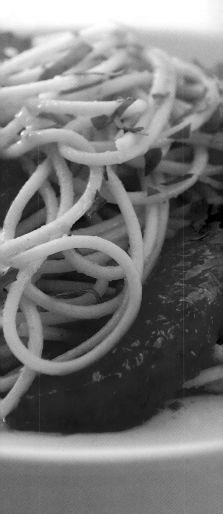

# Spaghetti
# **with butter, sage & bread crumbs**

| | |
|---|---|
| 1 | pound (500 g) spaghetti |
| $1/4$ | cup (60 g) butter |
| 1 | tablespoon extra-virgin olive oil |
| 3 | cloves garlic, finely chopped |
| $1/4$ | cup fresh sage leaves |
| 1 | cup (60 g) fresh bread crumbs |
| | Salt and freshly ground black pepper |
| | Freshly grated Parmesan cheese |

Cook the spaghetti in a large pot of salted boiling water until al dente.

While the pasta is cooking, heat the butter and oil in a medium frying pan over medium-high heat. Sauté the garlic and sage until pale gold, 2–3 minutes. Add the bread crumbs and cook, stirring from time to time, until crisp and golden, 3–5 minutes.

Drain the spaghetti and add to the pan. Season with salt and pepper. Toss well and serve hot with the Parmesan.

# Spaghettini
# **with lemon,**
# **chile & basil**

| | |
|---|---|
| 1 | pound (500 g) spaghettini or angel hair pasta |
| 1/2 | cup (125 ml) freshly squeezed lemon juice |
| 1/3 | cup (90 ml) extra-virgin olive oil |
| 2 | fresh red chiles, seeded and finely sliced |
| 3 | ounces (90 g) Parmesan cheese, freshly grated |
| 1 | cup fresh basil leaves |
| 2 | teaspoons finely grated lemon zest |
| | Salt and freshly ground black pepper |

Cook the pasta in a large pot of salted boiling water until al dente.

While the pasta is cooking, combine the lemon juice, oil, chiles, and Parmesan in a medium bowl. Whisk until well combined.

Drain the pasta and return to the pan. Add the lemon mixture, basil, and lemon zest. Season with salt and pepper. Toss well and serve hot.

# Spaghettini
# **with pesto, tomatoes & goat cheese**

| | |
|---|---|
| 1 | pound (500 g) spaghettini |
| 1 | pound (500 g) cherry tomatoes, halved |
| 1/2 | cup (125 ml) pesto, storebought or homemade (see page 26, made without the walnuts) |
| 3/4 | cup (180 g) caprino (soft Italian goat cheese) |
| | Freshly ground black pepper |

Cook the pasta in a large pot of salted boiling water until al dente.

Simmer the cherry tomatoes in the pesto in a large frying pan over medium heat until the tomatoes begin to soften, about 5 minutes.

Drain the pasta and add to the pan with the tomatoes.

Add the goat cheese and season with black pepper. Toss well and serve hot.

p. 96

Vegetable sauces are light
and nourishing and
perfect for family meals
and entertaining.

p. 150

p. 162

p. 126

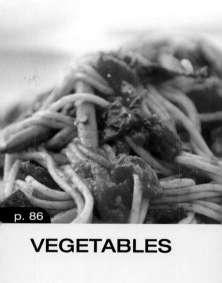

# VEGETABLES

# Vegetables

**Artichokes:** These winter vegetables go beautifully with pasta. To clean, begin by cutting off the top third of the leaves, then bend down and snap off all the tough outer leaves. Trim the stalk and cut the artichoke in half. Scrap out any fuzzy choke with a knife. Place in cold water with lemon juice to stop them turning brown.

**Arugula (Rocket):** This spicy salad plant grows wild in the Mediterranean area and has been popular in Italian cuisine since ancient Roman times.

**Bell Peppers (Capsicums):** Bell peppers, also known as capsicums, sweet peppers, or simply peppers, are from the same family as chilies. Plump and succulent, and rich in vitamins A and C and in carotenoids, they make an ideal addition to pasta salads. They are also delicious when grilled or gently braised and served in a hot pasta sauce.

**Broccoli:** Broccoli is a member of the cabbage family and is thought to have originated in Italy. There are now many varieties, ranging from green heads densely packed with florets, to the leafier sprouting broccoli, which can be green, purple, or white.

**Cauliflower:** From the same family as broccoli and botanically indistinguishable from it, many believe that cauliflowers originated in Cyprus, but no one really knows. Like broccoli, they are rich in vitamins and minerals and make a wonderful addition to pasta sauces.

**Eggplant (Aubergine):** Originally from India, eggplants are now popular around the world. They are much loved in Italian cuisine, where they are known as *melanzane* (from the Latin *mala insana*, meaning "the apple of madness").

**Fava Beans (Broad Beans):** These beans have been cultivated in Europe and Asia for thousands of years. They were a staple food for ancient Roman soldiers. Today, in central Italy, they are served raw in the early spring with fresh pecorino cheese, but also feature in many spring and summer pasta sauces.

**Peas:** An ancient legume, originally from the Near East, peas are eaten fresh or preserved by freezing or drying. High in fiber and a good source of protein, peas are always a healthy food choice.

**Tomatoes:** Originally from the Americas, tomatoes were taken to Europe by the Spaniards. The first known recipe comes from Naples and is for a tomato sauce made with finely chopped onion, parsley, garlic, oil, vinegar, salt, and pepper—not unlike many of our modern pasta sauces!

**Zucchini (Courgettes):** Zucchini, also known as courgettes in the UK and Australia and New Zealand, are part of the squash family. They have been popular in Italy since the 19th century, but only really caught on in North America and the UK in the 1950s and 60s, where they were probably introduced by Italian immigrants.

# Spaghetti **with sundried tomatoes & green beans**

| | |
|---|---|
| 1/4 | cup (60 ml) extra-virgin olive oil |
| 3 | cloves garlic, thinly sliced |
| 3 | ounces (90 g) sundried tomatoes, soaked in warm water for 15 minutes, drained, and coarsely chopped |
| 1 | (14-ounce/400-g) can tomatoes, with juice, chopped |
| 1 | pound (500 g) spaghetti |
| 12 | ounces (350 g) green beans, cut into short lengths |
| | Salt and freshly ground black pepper |

Heat the oil in a large frying pan over medium heat. Add the garlic and sundried tomatoes and sauté until the garlic is pale gold, 2–3 minutes.

Add the canned tomatoes and juice and simmer until the sauce is reduced, about 15 minutes.

Meanwhile, cook the pasta in a large pot of salted boiling water for 5 minutes. Add the beans and cook until the pasta is al dente.

Drain well and add to the pan with the sauce. Season with salt and pepper. Toss gently over high heat for 1 minute. Serve hot.

# Spaghetti
# **with fried eggplant & tomato**

| | |
|---|---|
| 1 | pound (500 g) eggplant (aubergine), with skin, thinly sliced |
| 2 | tablespoons coarse sea salt |
| 1 | cup (250 ml) olive oil, for frying |

Tomato Sauce

| | |
|---|---|
| 2 | pounds (1 kg) ripe tomatoes, peeled and coarsely chopped |
| 1 | onion, thinly sliced |
| 2 | cloves garlic, finely chopped |
| | Leaves from 1 small bunch basil, torn |
| 2 | tablespoons extra-virgin olive oil |
| 1/4 | teaspoon sugar |
| | Salt |

| | |
|---|---|
| 1 | pound (500 g) spaghetti |
| 1 | cup (125 g) freshly grated Parmesan cheese |

Place the eggplant in a colander and sprinkle with the coarse salt. Let drain for 1 hour.

Tomato Sauce: Stir the tomatoes, onion, garlic, basil, oil, sugar, and salt in a medium saucepan. Cover and simmer over medium heat for 15 minutes. Uncover and simmer over low heat until reduced, about 40 minutes. Chop in a food processor until smooth.

Heat the frying oil in a deep frying pan until very hot. Shake the salt off the eggplant and fry in small batches until tender, 5–7 minutes per batch. Drain on paper towels. Keep warm.

Cook the pasta in a large pot of salted boiling water until al dente. Drain and add to the sauce. Toss well and place on 4–6 individual serving plates. Top each portion with eggplant and sprinkle with Parmesan. Serve hot.

# Spaghetti
# **with tomato**
# **sauce**

| | |
|---|---|
| 3 | pounds (1.5 kg) ripe tomatoes, peeled and coarsely chopped |
| | Salt |
| 1 | onion, thinly sliced |
| 2 | cloves garlic, finely chopped |
| 10 | leaves fresh basil, torn |
| 3 | tablespoons extra-virgin olive oil |
| $1/2$ | teaspoon sugar |
| 1 | pound (500 g) spaghetti |

Simmer the tomatoes with the salt in a covered saucepan over medium heat for 5 minutes. Place in a colander and let drain for 1 hour.

Return the tomatoes to the saucepan and add the onion, garlic, basil, oil, sugar, and salt. Partially cover and simmer over low heat until the sauce is reduced, about 40 minutes. Remove from the heat and chop in a food processor until smooth.

Cook the spaghetti in a large pot of salted boiling water until al dente. Place in a heated serving bowl and toss with the sauce. Serve hot.

# Linguine
# **with tomatoes, paprika & olives**

| | |
|---|---|
| 1/3 | cup (90 ml) extra-virgin olive oil |
| 4 | cloves garlic, finely chopped |
| 2 | pounds (1 kg) ripe tomatoes, peeled and coarsely chopped |
| | Salt and freshly ground black pepper |
| 2 | tablespoons capers preserved in brine, drained |
| 1 1/2 | cups (150 g) pitted black olives, coarsely chopped |
| 1 | pound (500 g) linguine |
| 3 | tablespoons finely chopped fresh parsley |
| 1/2 | teaspoon hot paprika |

Heat the oil in a large frying pan over medium heat. Add the garlic and sauté until pale gold, 2–3 minutes.

Add the tomatoes and season with salt and pepper. Simmer for 10 minutes, then stir in the capers and olives. Simmer until reduced, 10–15 minutes.

Meanwhile, cook the pasta in a large pot of salted boiling water until al dente.

Drain and add to the pan with the sauce. Toss over high heat for 1 minute. Sprinkle with parsley and paprika and serve hot.

# Linguine
# **with spicy tomato sauce**

| | |
|---|---|
| $1/3$ | cup (90 ml) extra-virgin olive oil |
| 2 | cloves garlic, lightly crushed but whole |
| 2 | pounds (1 kg) ripe tomatoes, peeled and coarsely chopped |
| 1 | small dried chile, crumbled |
| 3 | drops Tabasco sauce |
| 1 | teaspoon hot paprika |
| | Salt |
| 1 | pound (500 g) linguine |
| $3/4$ | cup (90 g) freshly grated pecorino or Parmesan |

Heat the oil in a large frying pan over medium heat. Add the garlic and sauté until pale gold, 2–3 minutes. Discard the garlic.

Add the tomatoes and simmer until they begin to break down, about 25 minutes. Add the chile, Tabasco, and paprika. Season with salt.

Cook the pasta in a large pot of salted boiling water until al dente.

Drain and transfer to a serving dish. Sprinkle with the cheese. Add the sauce and toss well. Serve hot.

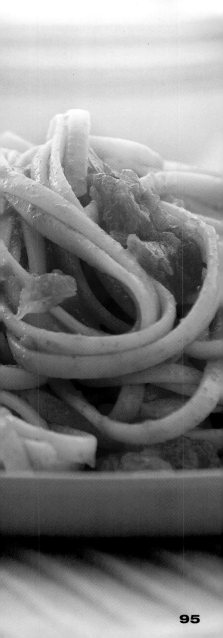

# Spaghetti
# **with summer vegetables**

| | |
|---|---|
| 5 | ounces (150 g) green beans, trimmed and cut in short lengths |
| 1 | pound (500 g) whole-wheat (wholemeal) spaghetti |
| 1/3 | cup (90 ml) extra-virgin olive oil |
| 1 | clove garlic, finely chopped |
| 2 | stalks celery, chopped |
| 20 | cherry tomatoes, quartered |
| 3 | small zucchini (courgettes), cubed |
| 1 | yellow bell pepper (capsicum), seeded and cut into small squares |
| 3 | ounces (90 g) arugula (rocket) |
| 1 | tablespoon white wine vinegar |
| | Salt and freshly ground black pepper |

Cook the green beans in a large pot of salted boiling water until tender, 5–7 minutes. Remove with a slotted spoon, reserving the cooking water.

Cook the pasta in the boiling water until al dente. Drain well. Transfer to a serving bowl and toss with 2 tablespoons of oil.

Add the garlic, green beans, celery, tomatoes, zucchini, bell pepper, arugula, the remaining oil, and the vinegar. Season with salt and pepper and toss well. Serve hot.

# Linguine
# **with pesto, potatoes & beans**

| | |
|---|---|
| 14 | ounces (400 g) green beans, chopped |
| 1 | pound (500 g) linguine |
| 8 | small new potatoes, cut into small cubes |
| 1 | quantity pesto (see page 26, made without the walnuts) |
| 2 | tablespoons extra-virgin olive oil |
| | Freshly ground black pepper |
| 1 | ounce (30 g) Parmesan cheese, cut into flakes |
| | Fresh basil leaves, to garnish |

Cook the green beans in a large pot of salted boiling water until almost tender, 5–7 minutes. Remove with a slotted spoon, reserving the cooking water.

Cook the linguine in the boiling water for 5 minutes. Add the potatoes and cook until the pasta is al dente and the potatoes are tender, 7–8 minutes. Drain well, reserving 3 tablespoons of the cooking liquid, and transfer to a large serving bowl.

Add the oil and the reserved cooking liquid to the pesto. Spoon over the pasta and potatoes, add the green beans, and toss well. Season with pepper. Sprinkle with the Parmesan. Garnish with basil and serve hot.

# Spaghetti
# **with button mushrooms**

| | |
|---|---|
| $1/3$ | cup (90 ml) extra-virgin olive oil |
| 2 | cloves garlic, finely chopped |
| $1^1/2$ | pounds (750 g) button mushrooms, sliced |
| | Salt and freshly ground black pepper |
| 8 | ounces (250 g) pancetta, cut into small pieces |
| 1 | pound (500 g) spaghetti |
| 2 | tablespoons finely chopped fresh parsley |
| 1 | cup (120 g) freshly grated pecorino or Parmesan |

Heat ¼ cup (60 ml) of oil in a large frying pan over medium heat. Add the garlic and sauté until pale gold, 2–3 minutes.

Add the mushrooms and sauté until tender, 7–10 minutes. Season with salt and pepper.

Heat the remaining oil in a small frying pan over medium heat. Add the pancetta and sauté until lightly browned and crisp, 3–4 minutes. Add the pancetta to the frying pan with the mushrooms. Mix well and simmer over low heat for 2 minutes.

Meanwhile, cook the pasta in a large pot of salted boiling water until al dente.

Drain the pasta and add to the pan with the mushrooms. Toss well, add the parsley, and season with pepper. Sprinkle with the cheese and serve hot.

# Spaghetti
# **with vegetable sauce**

| | |
|---|---|
| 1/3 | cup (90 ml) extra-virgin olive oil |
| 1 | large onion, finely chopped |
| 1 | carrot, finely chopped |
| 1 | stalk celery, chopped |
| | Salt and freshly ground black pepper |
| 2 | cloves garlic, sliced |
| 1 | tablespoon finely chopped fresh mint |
| 2 | pounds (1 kg) tomatoes, peeled and chopped |
| 1 | pound (500 g) spaghetti |
| 6 | tablespoons freshly grated pecorino cheese |

Heat the oil in a large frying pan over medium heat. Add the onion, carrot, and celery and season with salt and pepper. Cover and sweat over low heat for 10 minutes.

Add the garlic and mint and sauté over medium heat for 3 minutes. Stir in the tomatoes and simmer for 30 minutes. Season with salt.

Cook the pasta in a large pot of salted boiling water until al dente. Drain and add to the sauce. Add the pecorino and serve hot.

# Spaghetti
# with tomatoes
# & parmesan

| | |
|---|---|
| $^1/_3$ | cup (90 ml) extra-virgin olive oil |
| 4 | cloves garlic, finely chopped |
| 2 | stalks celery, sliced |
| 1 | small dried chile, crumbled |
| 2 | pounds (1 kg) ripe tomatoes, peeled and chopped |
| 2 | ounces (60 g) Parmesan cheese, in flakes |
| 2 | tablespoons chopped fresh cilantro (coriander) |

Heat the oil in a large frying pan over medium heat. Add the garlic, celery, and chile and sauté until the garlic is pale gold, 2–3 minutes.

Stir in the tomatoes and simmer for 15–20 minutes.

Meanwhile, cook the pasta in a large pot of salted boiling water until al dente.

Drain and add to the sauce. Add the cilantro and toss well. Top with the cheese and serve hot.

# Linguine
# **with mixed**
# **mushrooms**

| | |
|---|---|
| 1/4 | cup (60 ml) extra-virgin olive oil |
| 1 | large onion, finely chopped |
| | Salt |
| 2 | cloves garlic, finely chopped |
| 1 | dried chile, crumbled |
| 1/4 | cup (60 ml) dry white wine |
| 1 | pound (500 g) mixed small mushrooms (porcini, champignons, finferli/chanterelles, chiodini, etc), cleaned |
| 16 | cherry tomatoes, halved |
| | Leaves from 1 bunch fresh basil, torn |
| 2 | tablespoons finely chopped fresh parsley |
| 1 | pound (500 g) linguine |

Heat the oil in a large frying pan over low heat. Add the onion and sweat for 15 minutes.

Season with salt and add the garlic and chile. Pour in the wine and stir over medium heat until it evaporates. Add the mushrooms and sauté for a few minutes.

Stir in the tomatoes, basil, and parsley and simmer for about 10 minutes, or until the mushrooms are tender. Season with salt.

Meanwhile, cook the pasta in a large pot of salted boiling water until al dente.

Drain the pasta and add to the sauce. Toss well and serve hot.

# Spaghetti
# **with zucchini**

| | |
|---|---|
| 2 | cups (500 ml) extra-virgin olive oil + extra, to drizzle |
| 1 | pound (500 g) zucchini (courgettes), thinly sliced lengthwise |
| | Salt |
| 1 | pound (500 g) spaghetti |
| 1 | cup (120 g) coarsely grated pecorino or Parmesan |
| | Fresh basil, to garnish |

Heat the oil in a large deep frying pan until very hot. Fry the zucchini in batches until golden brown, 3–5 minutes per batch. Drain on paper towels. Season with salt and keep warm.

Cook the pasta in a large pot of salted boiling water until al dente.

Drain and place in a serving bowl. Top with cheese, zucchini, and basil, and a drizzle of extra oil. Serve hot.

# Bucatini
# with almonds, tomatoes & fried bread

- 1/4    cup (60 ml) extra-virgin olive oil
- 1      large onion, finely chopped
- 2      (14-ounce/400-g) cans tomatoes, with juice
         Salt and freshly ground black pepper
- 3      ounces (90 g) almonds
- 4      thick slices day-old firm-textured bread, cut in cubes
- 1      pound (500 g) bucatini
- 3/4    cup (75 g) pecorino cheese, in shavings

Heat 1 tablespoon of oil in a large frying pan over low heat. Add the onion and sweat for 10 minutes. Add the tomatoes and season with salt and pepper. Cover and simmer for 20–25 minutes.

Toast the almonds in a small frying pan over medium heat. Chop coarsely.

Sauté the bread in a large frying pan with the remaining oil until crisp and brown.

Cook the bucatini in a large pot of salted boiling water until al dente.

Drain the pasta and transfer to a heated serving bowl. Add the sauce, almonds, and bread. Toss well and top with the cheese. Serve hot.

# Bucatini
# **with artichokes & peas**

| | |
|---|---|
| 3 | artichokes, cleaned and sliced (see page 84 for instructions on how to clean artichokes) |
| | Freshly squeezed juice of 1 lemon |
| 1/4 | cup (60 ml) extra-virgin olive oil |
| 1 | onion, finely chopped |
| 8 | ounces (250 g) fresh peas |
| 1 | pound (500 g) fresh fava (broad) beans |
| | Salt and freshly ground white pepper |
| | Hot water, as required |
| | Leaves from 1 sprig fresh mint, finely chopped |
| 1 | tablespoon white wine vinegar |
| 1 | pound (500 g) bucatini |

Drizzle the artichokes with the lemon juice.

Heat the oil in a large frying pan over medium heat. Add the onion and sauté until softened, 3–4 minutes.

Add the peas, beans, and artichokes and season with salt and pepper. Cover and simmer over low heat, adding a little water from time to time to stop the sauce from drying out. Simmer until very tender, about 30 minutes.

Add the mint and vinegar and cook for 1 minute. Use a fork to mash some of the vegetables.

Meanwhile, cook the pasta in a large pot of salted boiling water until al dente. Drain and add to the vegetables. Toss well and serve hot.

# Linguine
# **with pesto & baked cherry tomatoes**

| | |
|---|---|
| 1$\frac{1}{2}$ | pounds (750 g) cherry tomatoes, cut in half |
| $\frac{1}{3}$ | cup (90 ml) extra-virgin olive oil |
| | Salt and freshly ground white pepper |
| 2 | ounces (60 g) fresh basil |
| $\frac{1}{2}$ | cup (60 g) freshly grated Parmesan cheese |
| 2 | cloves garlic, peeled |
| 1$\frac{1}{2}$ | ounces (45 g) shelled almonds |
| 1 | pound (500 g) linguine |

Preheat the oven to 350°F (180°C/gas 4). Place the cherry tomatoes on a baking sheet, cut side up, and drizzle with 2 tablespoons of oil. Season with salt and pepper. Bake for 15 minutes.

Chop the basil, Parmesan, garlic, almonds, and remaining oil in a food processor until smooth. Season with salt and pepper.

Cook the pasta in a large pot of salted boiling water until al dente.

Drain well and place in a heated serving dish. Add the pesto and baked tomatoes and toss gently. Serve hot.

# Spaghetti
# **Puglia style**

| | |
|---|---|
| 1/2 | cup (125 ml) extra-virgin olive oil |
| 2 | large fresh red chilies, whole |
| 2 | pounds (1 kg) San Marzano (oval) tomatoes, peeled, seeded, and cut in half lengthwise |
| | Salt and freshly ground black pepper |
| 1 | pound (500 g) spaghetti |
| | Fresh basil, torn |
| 1 | cup (120 g) freshly grated aged pecorino cheese |

Heat the oil in a large frying pan to very hot. Add the chilies and 1 tomato and fry for 2–3 minutes.

Add all the tomatoes one by one, cooking each one as you go. Season with salt and pepper and remove the chilies.

Cook the pasta in a large pot of salted boiling water until al dente.

Drain the pasta and add to the pan with the tomatoes. Add the basil and pecorino, toss well, and serve hot.

# Spaghetti
# with spicy cherry tomato sauce

| | |
|---|---|
| 2 | pounds (1 kg) cherry tomatoes, halved |
| 2 | cloves garlic, thinly sliced |
| 1/2 | teaspoon red pepper flakes or 1 small dried chile, crumbled |
| 1/2 | cup (125 ml) extra-virgin olive oil |
| | Salt and freshly ground black pepper |
| | Fresh basil leaves, torn |
| 1 | pound (500 g) spaghetti |

Place the tomatoes in a bowl with the garlic, pepper flakes, and basil.

Heat the oil in a large frying pan over high heat and add the contents of the bowl. Cook for 5–6 minutes, stirring with a wooden spoon at frequent intervals. Season with salt and remove from heat.

Meanwhile, cook the spaghetti in a large pot of salted boiling water until very al dente.

Drain and add to the pan. Toss over high heat until the sauce is absorbed by the pasta as it finishes cooking. Serve hot.

# Whole-wheat spaghetti
## with cheese & vegetables

| | |
|---|---|
| 1 | pound (500 g) whole-wheat (wholemeal) spaghetti |
| 1/2 | cup (125 ml) extra-virgin olive oil |
| 3 | medium zucchini (courgettes), diced |
| 3 | ounces (90 g) ricotta salata (or feta) cheese, diced |
| 3 | bell peppers (capsicums), cut in small squares |
| 3 | tablespoons finely chopped mixed fresh herbs (parsley, basil, marjoram, thyme) |
| | Salt and freshly ground white pepper |
| 1 | cup (100 g) pitted black olives |

Cook the pasta in a large pot of salted boiling water until al dente.

While the pasta is cooking, heat 3 tablespoons of oil in a large frying pan over medium heat. Add the zucchini and sauté for 3-4 minutes.

Drain the pasta into a heated serving bowl. Add the cheese, zucchini, and bell peppers. Season with the remaining oil, the herbs, salt, pepper, and olives. Toss well and serve hot.

# Linguine
# **with pumpkin and olives**

| 1 | pound (500 g) pumpkin (winter squash), peeled, seeded, and thinly sliced |
|---|---|
| 1/4 | cup (60 ml) extra-virgin olive oil |
| 1 | onion, finely chopped |
| | Salt and freshly ground black pepper |
| 1 | cup (100 g) pitted and chopped black olives |
| 1 | pound (500 g) linguine |
| 1/4 | cup (45 g) pine nuts, chopped |

Preheat the oven to 400°F (200°C/gas 6). Place the pumpkin in an ovenproof dish and roast for about 30 minutes, or until soft. Chop coarsely.

Heat 2 tablespoons of oil in a large frying pan over medium heat. Add the onion and sauté until softened, 3–4 minutes. Add the pumpkin and sauté until the pumpkin has broken down, 5–10 minutes. Season with salt and pepper and add the olives.

Meanwhile, cook the pasta in a large pot of salted boiling water until al dente. Drain, reserving 3 table-spoons of cooking water.

Add the pasta and reserved cooking water to the pan with the sauce. Toss gently. Add the pine nuts and drizzle with the remaining oil. Serve hot.

# Spaghetti **with bell pepper sauce**

<sup>1</sup>/<sub>3</sub>  cup (90 ml) extra-virgin olive oil

3  medium onions, thinly sliced

4  large ripe tomatoes, peeled and chopped

12  ounces (350 g) canned or bottled bell peppers (capsicums), drained

4  salt-cured anchovy fillets, finely chopped

 Salt

1  pound (500 g) spaghetti

Heat the oil in a large frying pan over medium heat. Add the onions and sauté until softened, 3-4 minutes.

Stir in the tomatoes and simmer until they begin to break down, about 10 minutes. Add the bell peppers and anchovies. Simmer for 5 minutes. Season with salt.

Meanwhile, cook the pasta in a large pot of salted boiling water until al dente.

Drain the pasta and add to the sauce. Toss well and serve hot.

# Spaghetti
# **Sicilian style**

- ¼ cup (60 ml) extra-virgin olive oil
- 1 small onion, finely chopped
- 1 clove garlic, lightly crushed but whole
- 2 pounds (1 kg) ripe tomatoes, peeled and finely chopped
- 12 leaves fresh basil, torn
- 1 sprig fresh oregano, finely chopped

  Salt and freshly ground black pepper
- 1 cup (100 g) black olives
- 2 tablespoons salt-cured capers, rinsed
- 1 pound (500 g) spaghetti

  Fresh parsley, to garnish

Heat the oil in a large frying pan over medium heat. Add the onion and garlic and sauté until pale gold, 2–3 minutes.

Stir in the tomatoes, basil, and oregano. Season with salt and pepper. Simmer for 5 minutes. Add the olives and capers. Simmer over low heat until the tomatoes have broken down, 10–15 minutes. Discard the garlic.

Meanwhile, cook the pasta in a large pot of salted boiling water until al dente.

Drain the pasta and add to the sauce. Toss well. Garnish with the parsley and serve hot.

# Spaghetti
## Naples style

| | |
|---|---|
| 1/3 | cup (90 ml) extra-virgin olive oil |
| 1 | small onion, finely chopped |
| 2 | (14-ounce/400-g) cans tomatoes, with juice |
| | Salt and freshly ground black pepper |
| 1 | tablespoon fresh basil, torn + extra, to garnish |
| 1 | pound (500 g) spaghetti |
| 3 | ounces (90 g) mozzarella cheese, cut in cubes |
| 3/4 | cup (90 g) freshly grated caciocavallo or Parmesan cheese |

Heat the oil in a large frying pan over medium heat. Add the onion and sauté until softened, 3–4 minutes.

Add the tomatoes and season with salt and pepper. Simmer for 15 minutes, then add the basil.

Meanwhile, cook the pasta in a large pot of salted boiling water until al dente.

Drain the pasta and add to the sauce. Toss over high heat for 1–2 minutes. Remove from the heat and add both cheeses. Garnish with the extra basil and serve hot.

# Bucatini
# **with sweet & sour sauce**

| | |
|---|---|
| 1 | small cauliflower, broken into florets |
| | Salt and freshly ground black pepper |
| 1 | pound (500 g) bucatini |
| $1/3$ | cup (90 ml) extra-virgin olive oil |
| 1 | onion, thinly sliced |
| 4 | salt-cured anchovy fillets |
| 4 | tablespoons golden raisins (sultanas) |
| 4 | tablespoons pine nuts |
| $1/4$ | teaspoon saffron, dissolved in 3 tablespoons hot water |
| 6 | tablespoons freshly grated pecorino cheese |

Cook the cauliflower in a large pot of salted boiling water until tender, about 5 minutes. Drain, reserving the cooking water.

Bring the water back to a boil and cook the pasta until al dente.

Heat the oil in a large frying pan over medium heat. Add the onion and sauté until softened, 3–4 minutes. Add the anchovies, raisins, pine nuts, and saffron mixture. Stir for 2–3 minutes, then add the cauliflower. Simmer over low heat.

Drain the pasta and add to the cauliflower mixture. Toss gently and sprinkle generously with pepper and pecorino. Serve hot.

# Spaghettini
# **with broccoli & gorgonzola**

| | |
|---|---|
| 1 | pound (500 g) broccoli, broken into florets |
| 1 | pound (500 g) spaghettini |
| $1/4$ | cup (60 ml) extra-virgin olive oil |
| 2 | cloves garlic, finely chopped |
| 8 | ounces (250 g) gorgonzola cheese, cubed |
| $1/2$ | cup (75 g) freshly grated Parmesan cheese |
| | Cracked pepper |

Cook the broccoli in a large pot of salted boiling water until tender, about 5 minutes. Drain, reserving the cooking water.

Bring the water back to a boil and cook the pasta until al dente.

While the pasta is cooking, heat the oil in a large frying pan over medium heat. Add the garlic and sauté until pale gold, 2–3 minutes. Add the broccoli to the pan and mix gently.

Drain the pasta and place in a heated serving bowl. Top with the broccoli, gorgonzola, and Parmesan. Season with cracked pepper. Toss gently and serve hot.

# Spicy spaghetti **with garlic mushrooms**

| | |
|---|---|
| 3 | tablespoons extra-virgin olive oil |
| 1 | pound (500 g) white mushrooms, thickly sliced |
| 4 | cloves garlic, thinly sliced |
| | Salt and freshly ground black pepper |
| 3 | tablespoons finely chopped fresh parsley |
| 1 | celery stalk, finely chopped |
| 1 | onion, finely chopped |
| 2 | (14-ounce/400-g) cans tomatoes, with juice |
| 1/2 | fresh red chile, seeded and finely chopped |
| 1 | pound (500 g) spaghetti |

Heat 1 tablespoon of oil in a large frying pan over high heat. Add the mushrooms and sauté until golden and softened, about 5 minutes.

Add the garlic and sauté for 1 minute. Season with salt and pepper. Transfer the mushroom mixture to a bowl with the parsley.

Add the onion and celery to the same pan with the remaining oil and sauté until lightly colored, about 5 minutes.

Stir in the tomatoes, chile, and salt. Simmer until reduced, about 15 minutes.

Meanwhile, cook the spaghettini in a large pot of salted boiling water until al dente. Drain and add to the sauce. Top with the mushrooms, toss gently, and serve hot.

# Spaghettini
# **with mint pea pesto**

| | |
|---|---|
| 8 | ounces (250 g) shelled fresh peas (about 2 pounds/1 kg in their pods) |
| 3 | cloves garlic, finely chopped |
| 2 | tablespoons pine nuts, toasted |
| 2 | ounces (60 g) Parmesan cheese, coarsely chopped + extra, freshly grated, to serve |
| 2 | sprigs fresh mint |
| $^1/_3$ | cup (90 ml) extra-virgin olive oil |
| | Salt and freshly ground black pepper |
| 1 | pound (500 g) spaghettini |

Cook the peas in salted boiling water until just tender, 2-3 minutes. Drain well.

Place the peas in a food processor with the garlic, pine nuts, Parmesan, mint, and oil. Season with salt and pepper, then pulse briefly until the ingredients are coarsely chopped.

Cook the spaghetti in a large pot of salted boiling water until al dente. Drain well, reserving some of the cooking water.

Place the spaghetti in a large serving bowl and add the pesto and enough of the reserved cooking water to make a moist sauce. Serve hot, with the extra Parmesan.

# Linguine
# **with broccoli, sesame & lime**

| | |
|---|---|
| 1 | pound (500 g) linguine |
| 1/4 | cup (60 ml) extra-virgin olive oil |
| 1 | pound (500 g) sprouting broccoli, trimmed and halved lengthways |
| 3 | fresh red chillies, seeded and thinly sliced lengthwise |
| 4 | cloves garlic, thinly sliced |
| 4 | tablespoons sesame seeds |
| 2 | tablespoons finely chopped fresh parsley |
| | Freshly squeezed juice of 2 limes |

Cook the pasta in a large pot of salted boiling water until al dente.

While the pasta is cooking, heat the oil in a large frying pan over medium-high heat. Add the broccoli and sauté for 5 minutes.

Add the chile and garlic and sauté until the broccoli is tender. Stir in the sesame seeds and sauté lightly browned.

Drain the pasta and add to the pan. Add the parsley and lime juice and toss well. Serve hot.

# Whole-wheat spaghetti **with spicy sauce**

| | |
|---|---|
| 1/3 | cup (90 g) extra-virgin olive oil |
| 2 | cloves garlic, finely chopped |
| 1 | large onion, finely chopped |
| 1 | fresh red chile, seeded and sliced |
| 6 | salt-cured anchovy fillets |
| 1 1/2 | pounds (750 g) ripe tomatoes, peeled and chopped |
| 3 | ounces (90 g) black olives, pitted |
| 2 | tablespoons salt-cured capers, rinsed |
| 1 | pound (500 g) whole-wheat (wholemeal) spaghetti |
| | Salt |

Heat the oil in a large frying pan over medium heat. Add the garlic, onion, and chile and sauté until softened, 3–4 minutes.

Add the anchovies and stir until they dissolve into the oil. Add the tomatoes, olives, and capers and simmer over low heat for 15–20 minutes.

Meanwhile, cook the spaghetti in a large pot of salted boiling water until al dente. Drain and add to the pan with the sauce. Toss over high heat for 1–2 minutes. Serve hot.

# Whole-wheat spaghetti **with onion & zucchini**

| | |
|---|---|
| 1/4 | cup (60 ml) extra-virgin olive oil |
| 2 | large white onions, sliced |
| 1 | fresh red chile, seeded and finely chopped |
| 1/4 | cup (60 ml) cold water |
| 4 | zucchini (courgettes), cut in small cubes |
| | Salt and freshly ground black pepper |
| 1 | pound (500 g) whole-wheat (wholemeal) spaghetti |
| 2 | ounces (60 g) Parmesan cheese, in flakes |
| 12 | fresh basil leaves, torn |

Heat the oil in a large frying pan over medium heat. Add the onions and chile and sauté for 2–3 minutes. Add the water and simmer until the water has evaporated.

Add the zucchini and simmer for 10–15 minutes more. Season with salt and pepper.

Meanwhile, cook the pasta in a large pot of salted boiling water until al dente. Drain the pasta, not too thoroughly, and add to the pan with the sauce. Toss over high heat until the water has evaporated. Add the Parmesan and basil and toss again. Serve hot.

# Linguine
# **with onion**
# **& pancetta**
# **sauce**

| | |
|---|---|
| 1/4 | cup (60 ml) extra-virgin olive oil |
| 1 1/2 | pounds (750 g) white onions, sliced |
| 3 | ounces (90 g) pancetta, diced |
| 2 | large tomatoes, diced |
| 1/2 | cup (125 ml) dry red wine |
| | Salt and freshly ground black pepper |
| 1 | pound (500 g) linguine |

Heat the oil in a large frying pan over medium heat. Add the onions and sauté until softened, 6–7 minutes.

Add the pancetta and sauté for 5 minutes more.

Add the tomatoes and then the wine. Season with salt and pepper. Cover and simmer over low heat for about 1 hour, stirring from time to time.

Cook the pasta in a large pot of salted boiling water until al dente.

Drain the pasta and add to the pan with the sauce. Toss gently and serve hot.

# Whole-wheat spaghetti **with onion sauce**

| | |
|---|---|
| 6 | large white onions, very thinly sliced |
| 1/3 | cup (90 ml) extra-virgin olive oil |
| | Salt and freshly ground black pepper |
| 1 | cup (250 ml) beef stock (homemade or bouillon cube) |
| 1 | pound (500 g) whole-wheat (wholemeal) spaghetti |
| | Finely chopped parsely, to garnish |

Place the onions in a heavy-bottomed pan with the oil over low heat. Season with a little salt (use less than you normally would because the very slow cooking enhances the taste of the salt). Add a grinding of pepper and cover.

Cook gently over very low heat for about 1 hour. The onions must not burn, but should slowly melt. Stir frequently, adding stock, as required, to keep the sauce moist. When cooked, the sauce should be creamy and golden.

Cook the pasta in a large pot of salted boiling water until al dente. Drain and place in a heated serving bowl. Add the onion sauce and parsley. Toss gently and serve hot.

# Spaghetti
## with zucchini flowers

| | |
|---|---|
| 1 | large white onion |
| 1 | bunch fresh parsley |
| 24 | zucchini (courgette) or squash flowers (reserve four to decorate) |
| 1/4 | cup (60 ml) extra-virgin olive oil |
| 2 | zucchini (courgettes), cut in small cubes |
| | Salt and freshly ground black pepper |
| | Pinch of saffron threads mixed with 1 tablespoon warm water |
| 3/4 | cup (180 ml) beef stock (homemade or bouillon cube) |
| 1 | pound (500 g) spaghetti |
| 1 | large egg yolk |
| 6 | tablespoons freshly grated pecorino cheese |

Finely chop the onion, parsley, and 20 zucchini flowers together.

Heat the oil in a large frying pan over medium heat. Add the onion mixture and zucchini and sauté for 3-4 minutes. Season with salt and pepper and add the saffron mixture. Simmer over low heat, adding stock as the mixture dries out, until the zucchini are tender, about 10 minutes.

Meanwhile, cook the pasta in a large pot of salted boiling water until al dente. Drain and add to the pan with the sauce. Stir in the egg yolk and 2 tablespoons of stock. Stir over low heat until the egg is cooked. Coarsely chop the reserved zucchini flowers. Sprinkle over the pasta with the cheese and serve hot.

# Homemade spaghetti **with garlic sauce**

1    quantity homemade
     spaghetti (see page 70)

Garlic Sauce

1/3  cup (90 ml) extra-virgin
     olive oil

10   cloves garlic, lightly
     crushed but whole

2    pounds (1 kg) ripe
     tomatoes, peeled,
     seeded, and finely
     chopped

1    small dried chile,
     crumbled (optional)

     Salt

Prepare the spaghetti.

Garlic Sauce: Heat the oil in a large frying pan over medium heat. Add the garlic and sauté until pale gold, 2–3 minutes.

Add the tomatoes and chile, if using, and season with salt. Simmer over low heat until the garlic has almost dissolved into the sauce, about 45 minutes.

Cook the pasta in a large pot of salted boiling water until al dente, 3–5 minutes.

Drain the pasta and add to the sauce. Toss gently and serve hot.

# Homemade spaghetti **with spicy tomato sauce**

1    quantity homemade spaghetti (see page 70)

Sauce

$^1/_3$    cup (90 ml) extra-virgin olive oil

2    cloves garlic, finely chopped,

1    tablespoon finely chopped fresh parsley

1    fresh red chile, seeded and finely chopped

2    pounds (1 kg) ripe tomatoes, peeled and coarsely chopped

     Salt

Prepare the spaghetti.

Sauce: Heat the oil in a large frying pan over medium heat. Add the garlic, parsley, and chile and sauté until the garlic is pale gold, 2–3 minutes.

Stir in the tomatoes and cook over medium heat until they have broken down, 10–15 minutes. Season with salt.

Meanwhile, cook the pasta in a large pot of salted boiling water until al dente, 3–5 minutes. Drain and add to the sauce. Toss well and serve hot.

# Homemade spaghetti
## with tomatoes & arugula

| | |
|---|---|
| 1 | quantity homemade spaghetti (see page 70) |

Sauce

| | |
|---|---|
| 5 | tablespoons extra-virgin olive oil |
| 2 | cloves garlic, sliced |
| 1 | small dried chile, crumbled |
| 1½ | pounds (750 g) tomatoes, peeled and chopped |
| 2 | large bunches arugula (rocket), finely shredded |
| 1 | stalk celery, chopped |
| 2 | ounces (60 g) Parmesan cheese, in flakes |
| 1 | tablespoon finely chopped fresh parsley |

Prepare the spaghetti.

Sauce: Heat the oil in a large frying pan over medium heat. Add the garlic and chile and sauté until the garlic is pale gold, 2–3 minutes.

Stir in the tomatoes and simmer over low heat for 15 minutes.

Cook the pasta in a large pot of salted boiling water until al dente.

Drain the pasta and add to the sauce. Add the arugula, celery, Parmesan, and parsley. Toss well and serve hot.

# Spaghetti
# **with cherry tomatoes & pancetta**

| | |
|---|---|
| 1 | pound (500 g) spaghetti |
| 1 | tablespoon extra-virgin olive oil |
| 5 | ounces (150 g) pancetta, coarsely chopped |
| 1 | pound (500 g) cherry tomatoes, halved |
| 3 | cloves garlic, crushed |
| 4 | tablespoons coarsely chopped fresh basil |
| | Salt and freshly ground black pepper |
| | Freshly grated Parmesan cheese, to serve |

Cook the spaghetti in a large pot of salted boiling water until al dente.

While the pasta is cooking, heat the oil in a large frying pan over medium-high heat. Sauté the pancetta until golden, 2–3 minutes. Add the tomatoes and garlic. Cook, stirring occasionally, until the tomatoes are soft, about 5 minutes.

Drain the pasta, reserving a little cooking water, and add to the pan. Add the basil and enough of the reserved cooking water to make a thick sauce. Season with salt and pepper. Toss well and serve hot with the cheese.

# Spaghetti
# **with zucchini & pine nuts**

| | |
|---|---|
| 1 | pound (500 g) spaghetti |
| 3 | tablespoons extra-virgin olive oil |
| $1/2$ | cup (90 g) pine nuts |
| 3 | tablespoons butter |
| 3 | cloves garlic, finely chopped |
| 3 | medium zucchini (courgettes), shredded or grated |
| 4 | tablespoons finely chopped fresh basil |
| $1/2$ | cup (125 ml) light (single) cream |
| | Salt and freshly ground black pepper |
| 1 | cup (125 g) freshly grated Parmesan cheese |

Cook the pasta in a large pot of salted boiling water until al dente.

While the pasta is cooking, heat 1 tablespoon of oil in a large frying pan over medium heat. Sauté the pine nuts until golden, about 1 minute. Remove with a slotted spoon.

Heat the remaining oil and the butter in the same pan. Sauté the garlic and zucchini until soft, 3–4 minutes.

Drain the pasta and place in the pan. Add the pine nuts, basil, and cream. Season with salt and pepper. Toss well and serve hot with the cheese.

# Spaghetti
# **with black olives & arugula**

| | |
|---|---|
| 1 | pound (500 g) linguine |
| 3 | cups (750 ml) homemade (see page 90) or storebought tomato-flavored pasta sauce |
| 1 | teaspoon sugar |
| 2 | bay leaves |
| | Salt and freshly ground black pepper |
| 1 | cup (100 g) small black olives |
| 3 | ounces (90 g) baby arugula (rocket) leaves |

Cook the linguine in a large pot of salted boiling water until al dente.

While the pasta is cooking, combine the tomato sauce, sugar, and bay leaves in a saucepan. Cover and simmer over low heat, stirring from time to time, for 10 minutes. Season with salt and pepper. Remove the bay leaves.

Drain the linguine and return to the pan. Add the tomato sauce, olives, and arugula. Toss well and serve hot.

# Bucatini
# **with broccoli**

1¼  pounds (600 g) broccoli,
      broken into small florets

1    pound (500 g) bucatini

3    tablespoons extra-virgin
      olive oil

6    scallions (green onions),
      finely chopped

2    tablespoons pine nuts

2    tablespoons raisins

1    cup (250 ml) dry white
      wine

¼   teaspoon saffron
      dissolved in ½ cup
      (125 ml) water

      Salt and freshly ground
      black pepper

5    salt-cured anchovy fillets

      Parmesan cheese,
      in flakes, to garnish

Cook the broccoli in a large
pot of salted boiling water
until tender, about 5
minutes. Drain, reserving

the cooking water. Bring the water back to a boil and cook the pasta until al dente.

While the pasta is cooking, heat 2 tablespoons of oil in a large frying pan over medium heat. Sauté the scallions until softened, 3–4 minutes. Add the pine nuts and raisins followed by the wine and cook until evaporated. Add the broccoli and saffron mixture. Season with salt and pepper. Simmer for 10 minutes.

Heat the remaining oil in a small saucepan over medium heat. Add the anchovies and stir until dissolved. Add to the broccoli mixture.

Drain the pasta and place in a serving bowl. Top with the broccoli and cheese, and serve hot

p. 168

Rich and creamy egg and cheese sauces make the ultimate comfort food pasta dishes.

p. 182

p. 194

p. 180

p. 184

# EGGS, CHEESE
# & CREAM

p. 192

p. 176

p. 170

# Eggs, Cheese & Cream

**Butter:** Is made by churning cream so that most of the water is forced out and the fat that is left clumps together. The final product is usually about 80 percent fat. Butter is not widely used in southern Italian cooking, where olive oil reigns supreme, but it is common in the north.

**Caciocavallo:** This cow's milk cheese has been made in southern Italy since medieval times. The distinctive pear-shape is created when the forms are hung to age or smoke. Caciocavallo is ideal for cooking, since it melts quickly and uniformly. When aged, it makes a tasty grating cheese.

**Caprino:** When fresh, this Italian goat cheese has a delicate flavor with a slight tang. When aged, the flavor becomes fairly sharp. Fresh caprino can be stirred into tomato or vegetable-based sauces, while the aged varieties are perfect for sprinkling.

**Carbonara:** This is the classic egg and pasta dish. It comes from Rome, where it is said to have been invented in the last days of World War II when allied troops arrived in the city with plentiful supplies of bacon.

**Cream:** Fresh cream is available with various levels of fat. Half and half cream is about 10–12 percent fat; light (single) cream is about 20 percent fat; heavy (double) cream can be up to 50 percent fat.

**Cream Cheese:** Is made from a mixture of milk and cream inoculated with lactic acid-producing bacteria which give the acidic taste.

**Gorgonzola:** This blue cheese takes its name from a village near Milan, where it has been made for centuries. Two types are made: *dolce*, which is creamy and pleasantly sharp, and *piccante*, which is crumblier and sharp.

**Mozzarella:** This fresh cheese comes from southern Italy, especially the area around Naples. Traditionally made from water buffalo's milk, most commercially produced mozzarella is now made from cow's milk.

**Parmesan:** Italy's best known cheese is made in northern Italy, in the area around Parma. Parmesan is made from skimmed cow's milk and is aged for 1–4 years before use.

**Pecorino:** Made from ewe's milk, pecorino is made all over Italy. It can be sweet when young and sharp when aged; there are many varieties.

**Provolone:** Made from whole cow's milk, this cheese is sweet and buttery when young and intense and spicy when aged. It is both a table and a cooking cheese.

**Ricotta:** Fresh ricotta is made from cow's or ewe's milk and lasts just a few days. Ricotta salata is made by adding salt to fresh ricotta and aging it for 2–12 months.

**Scamorza:** This sweet, buttery cheese is made in southern Italy. It also exists in a smoked version.

# Spaghetti
# **alla**
# **carbonara**

| | |
|---|---|
| 1 | pound (500 g) spaghetti |
| 1/4 | cup (60 ml) extra-virgin olive oil |
| 1 | onion, finely chopped |
| 1 1/3 | cups (150 g) diced bacon |
| 6 | large eggs |
| 1/3 | cup (90 ml) heavy (double) cream |
| | Salt and freshly ground black pepper |
| 3/4 | cup (90 g) freshly grated pecorino or Parmesan cheese |

Cook the pasta in a large pot of salted boiling water until al dente.

While the pasta is cooking, heat the oil in a small saucepan over medium heat. Add the onion and sauté until pale gold, 2–3 minutes. Add the bacon and sauté until crisp, about 5 minutes. Set aside.

Beat the eggs and cream in a large bowl. Season with salt and pepper and sprinkle with the cheese.

Drain the pasta and add to the pan with the bacon. Return to high heat, add the egg mixture, and toss briefly so that the eggs cook lightly but are still creamy. Serve immediately.

# Spaghetti
# with pancetta, mozzarella & egg

| | |
|---|---|
| ¹⁄₃ | cup (90 ml) extra-virgin olive oil |
| 3 | small eggplant (aubergines), cut into small cubes |
| 2 | cloves garlic, finely chopped |
| 1 | cup (125 g) pancetta or bacon, chopped |
| 2 | (14-ounce/400-g) cans tomatoes, with juice |
| 1 | fresh red chile, seeded and chopped |
| | Salt and freshly ground black pepper |
| 1 | pound (500 g) spaghetti |
| 4 | ounces (125 g) fresh mozzarella cheese, drained and cut into small cubes |
| 2 | large hard-boiled eggs, chopped |

Heat the oil in a large frying pan over medium heat. Add the eggplant and sauté until tender, about 10 minutes. Use a slotted spoon to transfer to paper towels. Let drain.

Add the garlic and pancetta to the frying pan and sauté until lightly browned, about 5 minutes. Stir in the tomatoes and chile and season with salt and pepper. Simmer over low heat until reduced, about 30 minutes.

Cook the pasta in a large pot of salted boiling water until al dente. Drain and add to the pan together with the mozzarella. Toss over high heat for 1 minute. Arrange the eggplant on top. Sprinkle with the egg and serve hot.

# Spaghettini
# **with ricotta & pecorino**

| 1 | pound (500 g) spaghettini |
|---|---|
| 1 | cup (250 g) fresh ricotta cheese, drained |
| $1/3$ | cup (90 g) butter, cut up |
| $1/2$ | cup (60 g) freshly grated ricotta salata cheese or other tasty aged grating cheese |
| 1 | small dried chile, crumbled |
| | Salt |
| $1/2$ | cup (60 g) freshly grated pecorino cheese |

Cook the pasta in a large pot of salted boiling water until al dente.

Mix the fresh ricotta, butter, ricotta salata, chile, and salt in a large bowl.

Drain the pasta, reserving 2 tablespoons of the cooking water. Transfer to the bowl with the ricotta mixture, adding the reserved cooking water.

Toss well, top with the pecorino, and serve hot.

# Spaghetti
# **with tomato & mozzarella**

| 1 | pound (500 g) spaghetti |
|---|---|
| 2 | pounds (1 kg) cherry tomatoes, cut in half |
| 8 | ounces (250 g) fresh mozzarella cheese, cut into small cubes |
| 2 | tablespoons finely chopped fresh basil |
| 1 | tablespoon finely chopped fresh mint |
| 1 | clove garlic, finely chopped |
| 1/2 | cup (125 ml) extra-virgin olive oil |
| | Salt and freshly ground black pepper |
| | Fresh basil leaves, to garnish |

Cook the pasta in a large pot of salted boiling water until al dente.

While the pasta is cooking, combine the tomatoes, mozzarella, basil, mint, garlic, and oil in a large bowl. Season with salt and pepper.

Drain the pasta and add to the bowl. Toss well. Garnish with the basil and serve hot.

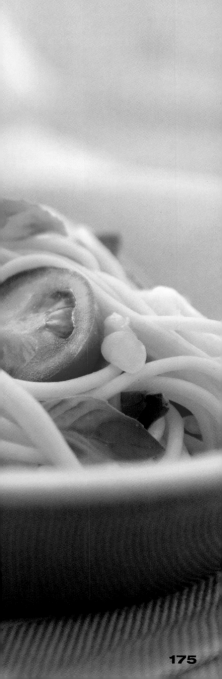

# Bucatini
# with eggs
# & artichokes

| | |
|---|---|
| 1/4 | cup (60 ml) extra-virgin olive oil |
| 1 | onion, finely chopped |
| 3 | ounces (90 g) pancetta, thinly sliced |
| 4 | artichokes, cleaned and thinly sliced (see page 84 for instructions on how to clean artichokes) |
| 1 | cup (250 ml) dry white wine |
| | Salt |
| 1 | cup (250 ml) water |
| 1 | pound (500 g) bucatini |
| 2 | large eggs |
| 1/2 | cup (60 g) freshly grated pecorino cheese |

Heat the oil in a large frying pan over medium heat. Add the onion and pancetta and sauté until pale golden brown, about 5 minutes.

Add the artichokes and simmer for 5 minutes. Add the wine and simmer until it has evaporated. Season with salt and add the water. Simmer until the artichokes are tender, 10–15 minutes.

Meanwhile, cook the pasta in a large pot of salted boiling water until al dente.

Beat the eggs in a small bowl with salt. Drain the pasta and add to the pan with the artichokes. Add the eggs and pecorino, toss over high heat for 1–2 minutes, and serve hot.

# Spaghetti
# **with cheese & pancetta**

| | |
|---|---|
| 6 | ounces (180 g) pancetta, cut in thin strips |
| 2 | cloves garlic, finely chopped |
| 5 | ounces (150 g) day-old bread, cut in cubes |
| 1/4 | cup (60 ml) extra-virgin olive oil |
| 1 | pound (500 g) spaghetti |
| 2 | tablespoons finely chopped fresh parsley |
| | Salt and freshly ground black pepper |
| 1 | cup (120 g) freshly grated pecorino cheese |

Heat the pancetta and garlic in a large non-stick frying pan over medium heat and sauté until crisp, about 5 minutes. Scoop the pancetta out of the pan and keep warm.

Place the bread in the pan with 2 tablespoons of oil and sauté until golden brown, about 5 minutes.

Meanwhile, cook the spaghetti in a large pot of salted boiling water until al dente.

Drain the pasta and add to the pan with the bread. Add the pancetta, parsley, remaining oil, and pecorino. Season with salt and pepper. Toss well and serve hot.

# Spaghetti
# **with pecorino, pancetta & leeks**

| | |
|---|---|
| 2 | tablespoons butter |
| 1/4 | cup (60 ml) extra-virgin olive oil |
| 1 | onion, finely chopped |
| 2 | cloves garlic, finely chopped |
| 4 | ounces (125 g) pancetta, diced |
| 10 | leeks, thinly sliced |
| 1 | cup (250 ml) boiling water |
| | Salt and freshly ground black pepper |
| 1 | pound (500 g) spaghetti |
| 2 | large egg yolks |
| | Dash of sugar |
| 6 | tablespoons freshly grated pecorino cheese |

Heat the butter and oil in a large frying pan over medium heat. Add the onion and garlic and sauté until pale gold, 3–4 minutes. Add the pancetta and sauté until crisp, about 5 minutes.

Add the leeks and boiling water and simmer over low heat until very tender, about 10 minutes. Season with salt and pepper.

Meanwhile, cook the spaghetti in a large pot of salted boiling water until al dente.

When the pasta is almost ready, beat the egg yolks and sugar in a small bowl. Add to the pan with the leeks and stir over medium-high heat for 1–2 minutes.

Drain the pasta and place in a heated serving dish. Toss with the sauce and sprinkle with pecorino. Serve hot.

# Whole-wheat spaghetti
## **with pear & gorgonzola**

| | |
|---|---|
| 1 | pound (500 g) whole-wheat (wholemeal) spaghetti |
| 1/4 | cup (60 g) butter |
| 12 | ounces (350 g) gorgonzola cheese, cut into small cubes |
| 1/3 | cup (90 ml) milk |
| | Salt |
| 1 | large ripe pear, peeled, cored, and cut into small cubes |
| | Coarsely chopped fresh parsley, to garnish |

Cook the pasta in a large pot of salted boiling water until al dente.

While the pasta is cooking, melt the butter in a medium saucepan over low heat. Add the gorgonzola and milk. Season with salt. Stir with a wooden spoon until the cheese has melted.

Add the pear and mix well.

Drain the pasta and place in a heated serving bowl. Add the cheese sauce and parsley. Toss well and serve hot.

# Spaghetti
# **with cream cheese & herbs**

| | |
|---|---|
| 1 | pound (500 g) spaghetti |
| 1/4 | cup (60 g) butter, softened |
| 1/2 | cup finely chopped fresh basil |
| 1/2 | cup finely chopped fresh parsley |
| 8 | ounces (250 g) cream cheese, softened |
| 1/2 | cup (60 g) freshly grated Parmesan cheese + extra, to serve |
| 1/4 | cup (60 ml) extra-virgin olive oil |
| 1 | clove garlic, finely chopped |
| | Freshly ground black pepper |
| 1/2 | cup (125 ml) boiling water |

Cook spaghetti in a large pot of boiling salted water until al dente.

While the pasta is cooking, combine the butter, basil, parsley, cream cheese, Parmesan, oil, and garlic in a bowl.

Season with a generous amount of black pepper. Stir in the boiling water until the mixture is smooth and well combined.

Drain the pasta and place in a heated serving bowl. Spoon half the sauce over the top. Serve the remainder separately with the extra Parmesan.

# Spaghetti
## with peas, bacon & parmesan

| | |
|---|---|
| 1 | pound (500 g) spaghetti |
| 1 | tablespoon extra-virgin olive oil |
| 6 | ounces (180 g) bacon slices, coarsely chopped |
| 1 | onion, finely chopped |
| 1/2 | cup (125 ml) chicken stock (homemade or bouillon cube) |
| 1 | cup (150 g) frozen peas |
| 2 | tablespoons finely chopped fresh mint |
| 5 | ounces (150 g) Parmesan cheese, coarsely grated |
| | Salt and freshly ground black pepper |

Cook the spaghetti in a large pot of salted boiling water until al dente.

While the pasta is cooking, heat the oil in a large frying pan over medium heat. Add the bacon and onion and sauté until the bacon is crisp, about 5 minutes. Remove from the pan and keep warm.

Add the chicken stock to the pan and bring to a boil. Add the peas and mint. Cover and simmer until tender, 2–3 minutes.

Drain the pasta and add to the pan with the pea mixture. Add the bacon mixture and Parmesan. Season with salt and pepper. Toss well and serve hot.

# Spaghetti with cherry tomatoes & mozzarella

| 1 | pound (500 g) spaghetti |
| $^{1}/_{3}$ | cup (90 ml) extra-virgin olive oil |
| 1 | tablespoon finely chopped fresh oregano |
| 1 | small dried chile, crumbled |
| 2 | cloves garlic, lightly crushed but whole |
| 2 | pounds (1 kg) cherry tomatoes, halved |
| | Salt |
| 8 | ounces (250 g) small mozzarella balls (bocconcini), halved |

Cook the spaghetti in a large pot of salted boiling water until al dente.

While the pasta is cooking, mix the oil, oregano, chile, and garlic in a small bowl.

Heat a large frying pan over medium heat. Add the oil mixture and sauté until the garlic is pale gold, 2-3 minutes. Add the tomatoes and sauté for 3 minutes.

Drain the pasta and add to the pan with the tomatoes. Season with salt. Add the mozzarella and toss well. Serve hot.

# Linguine
## alla carbonara

| | |
|---|---|
| 1 | pound (500 g) linguine |
| 8 | slices bacon, thinly sliced |
| 4 | large eggs |
| 1¼ | cups (300 ml) light (single) cream |
| ½ | cup (60 g) freshly grated Parmesan cheese |

Cook the linguine in a large pot of salted boiling water until al dente.

While the pasta is cooking, dry-fry the bacon in a large frying pan over medium heat until crisp, about 5 minutes. Set aside.

Beat the eggs with the cream and Parmesan in a medium bowl. Add the bacon.

Drain the linguine and return to the pan. Pour in the egg mixture and cook over low heat until the sauce begins to thicken and the eggs are cooked through, about 2 minutes. Toss well and serve hot.

# Linguine
# **with butter**
# **& cream**

| | |
|---|---|
| 1 | pound (500 g) linguine |
| $1/3$ | cup (90 g) butter, cut up |
| $1^1/4$ | cups (300 ml) light (single) cream |
| $1/2$ | cup (60 g) freshly grated Parmesan cheese |
| 3 | tablespoons finely chopped fresh parsley |

Cook the linguine in a large pot of salted boiling water until al dente.

While the pasta is cooking, melt the butter in a large frying pan over low heat. Add the cream and cheese and simmer over low heat for 4 minutes. Stir in the parsley.

Drain the pasta and add to the pan with the sauce. Toss well and serve hot.

# Linguine
# **with walnuts & gorgonzola**

1     pound (500 g) linguine

$^1/_3$     cup (90 ml) apple cider vinegar

1     cup (125 g) walnuts, toasted

12     ounces (350 g) baby spinach leaves, tough stems removed

8     ounces (250 g) gorgonzola cheese, crumbled

Cook the linguine in a large pot of salted boiling water until al dente.

While the pasta is cooking, heat the apple cider vinegar and walnuts in a medium saucepan.

Drain the pasta well and return to the pan. Pour the apple cider mixture over the linguine and add the spinach and cheese. Toss well and serve hot.

p. 212

Seafood sauces are tasty, elegant, and healthy. Here you will find more than 30 brilliant recipes.

p. 220

p. 248

p. 256

# SEAFOOD

# Seafood

**Anchovies:** Fresh anchovies are not always readily available. Our recipes call for preserved (salt-cured) anchovy fillets that are widely available in cans or jars. They have a strong, salty taste and add flavor and zest to sauces.

**Calamari:** This is the Italian name for squid.

**Caviar:** This luxury food is made from the salted roe (eggs) of certain species of fish, usually the sturgeon (black caviar) and the salmon (red caviar).

**Clams:** There are many different species of clams. From the same group as mussels and scallops, they are best bought live in the shell. Soak them in a large bowl of cold water for an hour or two—changing the water often—before use.

**Crabs:** There are dozens of species of crab. Crabs can be bought live, pre-cooked, chilled, or frozen. Their white meat is deliciously sweet.

**Crayfish:** These are not the freshwater crawfish of North America, but a type of spiny lobster found mainly in Mediterranean waters. Replace with lobster or large shrimp.

**Cuttlefish:** From the same family as squid and octopus, cuttlefish live in the Mediterranean and Atlantic Ocean. They are very similar to squid, so substitute with squid if you can't find them.

**Lobster:** Sweet, fresh lobster meat is always a treat. Lobsters are often available ready-cooked so you only need to split them in two with a sharp knife to remove the meat. Fresh lobsters are alive; they are usually cooked by plunging them into boiling water.

**Mussels:** These edible bivalves thrive on rocks, piers, pilings, and anywhere else they can gain anchor in calm seawater. Buy fresh in the shell and soak in cold water for an hour or two. You may also need to scrub them with a wire brush to remove the "beards" from their shells.

**Salmon:** Now available year round from salmon farms, this is one of the best fish you can buy. Smoked salmon is also delicious.

**Sardines:** Usually available in cans, fresh sardines are delicious—when you can find them. They become rancid quickly; sniff them before buying—there should be little or no odor.

**Scallops:** Unlike mussels, scallops are usually bought already shucked. They should smell sweet and not show any browning.

**Shrimp (Prawns):** There are thousands of species of shrimp, from small to jumbo. If you can, buy them fresh; if unavailable, buy frozen (rather than thawed).

**Squid:** Also known as calamari and inkfish, squid freezes well, so don't worry if it's not available fresh. To avoid rubbery texture, either cook it really fast over high heat or braise slowly for 45–60 minutes.

**Tuna:** Canned tuna is the most popular fish on the market and makes a great pasta sauce. Fresh tuna is tender, flavorful, easy to prepare, and completely devoid of fat.

# Spaghetti
# **with black olives & anchovies**

| 1/3 | cup (90 ml) extra-virgin olive oil |
|---|---|
| 1 | red onion, chopped |
| 1–2 | small dried chilies, crumbled |
| 3 | cloves garlic, finely chopped |
| 4 | salt-cured anchovy fillets |
| 1 1/2 | pounds (750 g) ripe tomatoes, peeled and finely chopped |
| 1 | cup (100 g) black olives |
| 1 | tablespoon salt-cured capers, chopped |
| 1 | pound (500 g) spaghetti |
| 1 | tablespoon finely chopped fresh parsley |

Heat the oil in a large frying pan over medium heat. Add the onion and chilies and sauté until softened, 3–4 minutes.

Add the garlic and anchovies and sauté over low heat, crushing the anchovies with a fork until they have dissolved into the oil, about 5 minutes.

Stir in the tomatoes and simmer for 15 minutes. Add the olives and capers and simmer for 5 more minutes.

Meanwhile, cook the pasta in a large pot of salted boiling water until al dente.

Drain the pasta and add to the sauce. Sprinkle with the parsley, toss well, and serve hot.

# Spaghetti
# **with clams**
# **& mussels**

| | |
|---|---|
| 1½ | pounds (750 g) clams, in shell |
| 1½ | pounds (750 g) mussels, in shell |
| ⅔ | cup (150 ml) dry white wine |
| 4 | cloves garlic, finely chopped |
| 1 | small dried chile, crumbled |
| ⅓ | cup (90 ml) extra-virgin olive oil |
| 1 | pound (500 g) spaghetti |
| 2 | tablespoons butter, cut up |
| 2 | tablespoons finely chopped fresh parsley |

Soak the shellfish in a large bowl of cold water for 1 hour. Drain and rise well.

Place the shellfish in a large pan with half the

wine. Cover and cook over high heat until open, 5–10 minutes. Discard any that do not open. Remove about half the mollusks from their shells. Set the cooking liquid aside.

Heat the remaining oil in a large frying pan over medium heat. Add the garlic and chile and sauté until pale gold, 2–3 minutes.

Add the shellfish and simmer for 2 minutes. Pour in the remaining wine and cook until it evaporates.

Cook the pasta in a large pot of salted boiling water until al dente. Drain and add to the sauce, adding a little of the strained cooking liquid. Toss with the butter and sprinkle with the parsley. Serve hot.

# Spaghetti
# **with spicy clam sauce**

| | |
|---|---|
| 2 | pounds (1 kg) clams, in shell |
| 1/3 | cup (90 ml) extra-virgin olive oil |
| 4 | cloves garlic, finely chopped |
| 1 | fresh red chile, seeded and chopped |
| 6 | large tomatoes, sliced |
| 1/2 | cup (125 ml) dry white wine |
| | Salt |
| 1 | pound (500 g) spaghetti |
| 3 | tablespoons finely chopped fresh parsley |

Soak the clams in cold water for 1 hour.

Place the clams in a large pan over medium heat with a little water. Cook until they open, 5–10 minutes. Discard any that do not open. Remove from the heat and discard most of the shells. Leave a few in their shells to garnish.

Heat the oil in a large frying pan over medium heat. Add the garlic and chile and sauté until pale gold, 2–3 minutes.

Add the tomatoes and wine, season with salt, and simmer until the tomatoes begin to break down, about 15 minutes. Add the clams and stir well.

Meanwhile, cook the pasta in a large pot of salted boiling water until al dente. Drain and add to the pan with the clams. Toss well. Sprinkle with the parsley and serve hot.

# Seafood spaghetti **en papillote**

| | |
|---|---|
| 1$^1$/$_2$ | pounds (750 g) clams, in shell |
| 1$^1$/$_2$ | pounds (750 g) mussels, in shell |
| $^1$/$_3$ | cup (90 ml) extra-virgin olive oil |
| 2 | cloves garlic, finely chopped |
| 1 | small dried chile, crumbled |
| 2 | tablespoons finely chopped fresh parsley |
| $^1$/$_2$ | cup (125 ml) dry white wine |
| 1$^1$/$_2$ | pounds (750 g) firm-ripe tomatoes, peeled and chopped |
| 14 | ounces (400 g) small squid, cleaned |
| 12 | ounces (350 g) shelled crayfish |
| 1 | pound (500 g) spaghetti |
| | Salt |

Soak the clams and mussels in a large bowl of cold water for 1 hour. Drain and set aside.

Preheat the oven to 350°F (180°C/gas 4). Heat the oil in a small saucepan over medium heat. Add the garlic, chile, and parsley and sauté until the garlic is pale gold, 2–3 minutes.

Pour in the wine and simmer until it evaporates. Add the tomatoes and simmer for 10 minutes.

Add the squid, clams, mussels, and crayfish. Cover and simmer over medium heat until the clams and mussels open up. Remove from the heat and discard any clams or mussels that haven't opened. Shell half the shellfish.

Meanwhile, cook the spaghetti in a large pot of salted boiling water for half the time indicated on the package.

Drain the pasta and add to the seafood sauce.

Cut 4–6 large pieces of aluminum foil or parchment paper and fold each one in half to double the thickness.

Divide the pasta into 4–6 portions and place in the center of the pieces of foil or paper, adding 2 tablespoons of cooking water from the pasta to each portion. Close, sealing well. There should be a small air pocket in each of the packages.

Bake until puffed up slightly, 12–15 minutes.

Place the packages on individual serving dishes; your guests can open and eat directly from them.

# Spaghetti
# **with tuna**
# **& cherry**
# **tomatoes**

| | |
|---|---|
| 1/4 | cup (60 ml) extra-virgin olive oil |
| 2 | cloves garlic, finely chopped |
| 8 | ounces (250 g) canned tuna, drained and crumbled |
| 1/3 | cup (90 ml) dry white wine |
| 1 | pound (500 g) cherry tomatoes, halved |
| | Salt and freshly ground white pepper |
| 1 | pound (500 g) spaghetti |
| 1 | tablespoon finely chopped fresh parsley |

Heat the oil in a large frying pan over medium heat. Add the garlic and sauté until pale gold, 2–3 minutes.

Add the tuna and sauté briefly. Pour in the wine and cook until evaporated.

Add the tomatoes. Season with salt and pepper and simmer for 15 minutes.

Meanwhile, cook the pasta in a large pot of salted boiling water until al dente.

Drain the pasta and transfer to serving bowls. Top with the hot sauce. Sprinkle with parsley and serve hot.

# Spaghetti
# **with squid's ink**

| | |
|---|---|
| 1 | pound (500 g) squid or cuttlefish, cleaned, with ink sacs |
| 1/4 | cup (60 ml) extra-virgin olive oil |
| 2 | cloves garlic, finely chopped |
| | Leaves from 1 small bunch parsley, finely chopped + extra, to garnish |
| 1 | small dried chile, crumbled |
| 1 | tablespoon tomato paste (concentrate) |
| 1/3 | cup (90 ml) white wine |
| | Salt |
| 1/3 | cup (90 ml) hot water |
| 1 | pound (500 g) spaghetti |

Cut the squid bodies into rings and chop the tentacles into small pieces.

Heat the oil in a medium saucepan over medium heat. Add the garlic and sauté until pale gold, 2–3 minutes. Add the squid, parsley, and chile.

Dissolve the tomato paste in 3 tablespoons of wine and add to the saucepan. Season with salt and add the hot water. Cover and simmer until the squid is tender, 45–50 minutes.

Remove the ink from the bladders and mix with the remaining wine. Stir into the sauce a few minutes before serving.

Meanwhile, cook the pasta in a large pot of salted boiling water until al dente. Drain and toss with the sauce. Garnish with the extra parsley and serve hot.

# Spaghetti
# **with tuna & capers**

| | |
|---|---|
| 1 | pound (500 g) spaghetti |
| 4 | tablespoons salt-cured capers |
| 8 | ounces (250 g) canned tuna, drained |
| | Leaves from 1 bunch fresh mint |
| 1 | small dried chile, crumbled (optional) |
| 5 | tablespoons extra-virgin olive oil |
| | Salt |

Cook the pasta in a large pot of salted boiling water until al dente.

While the pasta is cooking, rinse the capers under cold running water and cover with fresh water in a small saucepan. Place over medium heat. Bring to a boil, drain, rinse again, and dry on paper towels.

Mix the tuna, capers, mint, and chile, if using, in a large bowl. Mix in the oil. Season with salt.

Drain the pasta, reserving 2–3 tablespoons of the cooking water. Add the pasta and reserved cooking water to the bowl with the tuna sauce. Toss well and serve hot.

# Spaghetti
# **with lobster**

| | |
|---|---|
| ¹/₄ | cup (60 ml) extra-virgin olive oil |
| 1 | onion, finely chopped |
| 1 | tablespoon finely chopped fresh parsley |
| 1 | pound (500 g) tomatoes, peeled and chopped |
| | Salt |
| 14 | ounces (400 g) fresh lobster meat, cut into large chunks |
| 1 | pound (500 g) spaghetti |

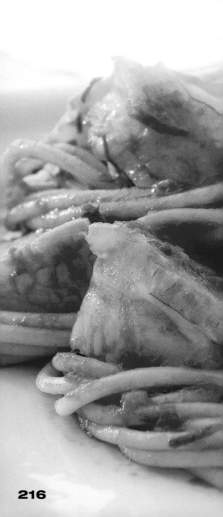

Heat the oil in a large frying pan over low heat. Add the onion and sweat for 10 minutes.

Add the parsley and tomatoes. Simmer until the tomatoes have broken down, 15–20 minutes. Season with salt and add the lobster meat. Simmer for 5 minutes.

Cook the pasta in a large pot of salted boiling water until al dente.

Drain and add to the pan with the lobster sauce. Toss gently and serve hot.

# Spaghetti
# **with calamari**

| | |
|---|---|
| 1/4 | cup (60 ml) extra-virgin olive oil |
| 2 | onions, finely chopped |
| 2 | cloves garlic, finely chopped |
| 12 | baby calamari, cleaned |
| 2 | (14-ounce/400-g) cans tomatoes, with juice |
| | Salt and freshly ground black pepper |
| 1 | pound (500 g) spaghetti |

Heat the oil in a large frying pan over medium heat. Add the onion and garlic and sauté until they begin to change color, 3-4 minutes.

Add the calamari and tomatoes. Season with salt and pepper. Turn the heat down low, cover, and simmer until the calamari are tender, about 45 minutes.

Cook the spaghetti in a large pot of salted boiling water until al dente.

Drain the pasta and place in a heated serving dish. Toss with the sauce and serve hot.

# Spaghetti
# **with scampi**
# **& olive pesto**

| | |
|---|---|
| 6 | tablespoons pine nuts |
| 1 | cup (100 g) pitted black olives |
| | Large bunch fresh parsley |
| $^{1}/_{2}$ | cup (125 ml) extra-virgin olive oil |
| | Salt and freshly ground black pepper |
| 12 | scampi, shelled, deveined, and chopped |
| 1 | clove garlic, finely chopped |
| 1 | pound (500 g) spaghetti |

Place the pine nuts in a large frying pan over medium-high heat and toast until golden brown.

Chop almost all the olives (reserve a few whole to garnish), 4 tablespoons of pine nuts, the parsley, and 5 tablespoons of oil in a food processor until smooth. Season with salt and pepper.

Heat the remaining oil in a large frying pan over high heat. Add the scampi and garlic and sauté for 5 minutes.

Meanwhile, cook the spaghetti in a large pot of salted boiling water until al dente.

Drain well and add to the pan with the scampi. Add the pesto, reserved olives, and remaining pine nuts and toss gently. Serve hot.

# Spaghetti
# **with tuna, tomatoes & cilantro**

| | |
|---|---|
| 1 | pound (500 g) spaghetti |
| 3 | tablespoons extra-virgin olive oil |
| 3 | cloves garlic, finely chopped |
| 1/2 | teaspoon sugar |
| 2 | tablespoons finely chopped fresh cilantro (coriander) |
| 1 | small dried chile, crumbled |
| 1 | pound (500 g) cherry tomatoes, halved |
| | Salt and freshly ground black pepper |
| 1 | (14-ounce/400-g) can tuna, drained and crumbled |

Cook the spaghetti in a large pot of salted boiling water until al dente.

While the pasta is cooking, heat the oil in a large frying pan over medium heat. Add the garlic, sugar, cilantro, and chile and sauté until the garlic is pale gold, 2–3 minutes.

Add the tomatoes, season with salt, and simmer for 5 minutes. Add the tuna, stir well, then turn off the heat immediately.

Drain the pasta and transfer to a heated serving dish. Toss gently with the sauce and serve hot.

# Bucatini
# **with**
# **swordfish**
# **& herbs**

| | |
|---|---|
| 1 | large thick slice of swordfish, weighing about 1 pound (500 g) |
| | Freshly squeezed juice of 2 lemons |
| 1/3 | cup (90 ml) extra-virgin olive oil |
| 2 | cloves garlic, finely chopped |
| 2 | tablespoons finely chopped fresh parsley |
| 1 | teaspoon fennel seeds, lightly crushed |
| 1 | fresh red chile, sliced |
| 4 | tablespoons pistachios |
| | Salt |
| 1 | pound (500 g) bucatini |

Clean the swordfish, removing the skin and the large central bone. Cut into bite-sized pieces.

Place in a large flat-bottomed bowl and drizzle with the lemon juice. Set aside for 5 minutes.

Heat the oil in a large frying pan over medium heat. Add the garlic, parsley, fennel seeds, and chile and sauté for 3–4 minutes.

Add the swordfish and pistachios. Season with salt and sauté over high heat until tender, 3–5 minutes.

Meanwhile, cook the pasta is a large pot of salted boiling water until al dente.

Drain the pasta and add to the pan with the sauce. Toss gently and serve hot.

# Bavette
# **with salmon & lime**

| | |
|---|---|
| 1 | pound (500 g) bavette |
| 1/4 | cup (60 ml) extra-virgin olive oil |
| 2 | cloves garlic, finely chopped |
| 1 | fresh red chile, seeded and finely chopped |
| 1 | tablespoon finely chopped fresh parsley |
| 14 | ounces (400 g) fresh salmon fillets, cut in thin strips |
| | Freshly squeezed juice and finely grated zest of 1 lime |
| | Salt and freshly ground black pepper |

Cook the pasta in a large pot of salted boiling water until al dente.

While the pasta is cooking, heat the oil in a large frying pan over high heat. Sauté the garlic, chile, and parsley until the garlic is pale gold, 2–3 minutes. Add the salmon and sauté until tender, 3–5 minutes.

Drain the pasta and add to the pan. Add the lime juice and zest and season with salt and pepper. Toss gently and serve hot.

# Spaghetti
# **with seafood**

| | |
|---|---|
| 12 | ounces (350 g) mussels in shell |
| 12 | ounces (350 g) squid, cleaned |
| 12 | ounces (350 g) cuttlefish |
| 12 | ounces (350 g) shrimp (prawn) tails |
| $^1/_2$ | cup (125 ml) extra-virgin olive oil |
| 4 | cloves garlic, finely chopped |
| 3 | tablespoons finely chopped fresh parsley |
| $^1/_2$ | cup (125 ml) dry white wine |
| | Salt and freshly ground black pepper |
| 1 | pound (500 g) spaghetti |

Soak the mussels in a large bowl of cold water for at least an hour, changing the water often.

Chop the squid and cuttlefish bodies into rounds and the tentacles into short pieces.

Do not peel the shrimp tails.

Pour 3 tablespoons of the oil into a large frying pan, add the mussels and clams, and cook over medium heat until opened, 5–10 minutes. Discard any that have not opened.

Heat the remaining oil in a large frying pan over medium heat. Add the garlic and parsley and sauté until the garlic is pale gold, 2–3 minutes. Add the squid and cuttlefish. Season with salt and pepper, cook briefly, then add the wine. Simmer over low heat until the squid and cuttlefish are tender, about 45 minutes.

Add the shrimp tails, clams and mussels and simmer over medium heat until the seafood is cooked, 3–5 minutes. If preferred, extract the mussels and clams from their shells, leaving just a few in the shell to make the finished dish look more attractive.

Meanwhile, cook the spaghetti in a large pot of salted boiling water until al dente. Drain and add to the pan with the seafood sauce. Toss well and serve hot.

# Spaghetti
# **with shellfish, scampi & squid**

| | |
|---|---|
| 12 | ounces (350 g) mussels, in shell |
| 12 | ounces (350 g) clams, in shell |
| 1/3 | cup (90 ml) extra-virgin olive oil |
| 2 | cloves garlic, finely chopped |
| 4 | tablespoons finely chopped fresh parsley |
| 1–2 | small dried chilies, crumbled |
| 12 | ounces (350 g) squid, cleaned, and cut into bite-sized chunks |
| 12 | ounces (350 g) scampi |
| 1/4 | cup (60 ml) dry white wine |
| | Salt and freshly ground black pepper |
| 1 | pound (500 g) spaghetti |

Soak the mussels and clams in a large bowl of cold water for at least an hour, changing the water often.

Heat 3 tablespoons of the oil in a large frying pan over medium heat. Add the shellfish and simmer until opened. Discard any that do not open. Extract the mollusks. Leave a few in their shells to garnish.

Heat the remaining oil in a large frying pan over high heat. Add the garlic, parsley, chile, squid, scampi, mussels, and clams. Sauté very quickly, until the squid is just tender. Add the wine, season with salt and pepper and remove from the heat.

Meanwhile, cook the spaghetti in a large pot of salted boiling water until al dente. Drain and add to the pan. Toss over high heat and serve hot.

# Spaghetti
# **with vodka**
# **& caviar**

- 1     pound (500 g) spaghetti
- 1/4    cup (60 g) butter
- 1/4    cup (60 ml) vodka
-        Freshly squeezed juice of 1 1/2 lemons
- 4     ounces (125 g) smoked salmon, crumbled
- 4     teaspoons caviar
- 1/4    cup (60 ml) light (single) cream
-        Salt and freshly ground black pepper

Cook the spaghetti in a large pot of salted boiling water until al dente.

While the pasta is cooking, melt the butter in a large frying pan over medium-low heat. Add the vodka and lemon juice and simmer for 1–2 minutes.

Add the salmon and caviar and simmer for 2–3 minutes. Add the cream and season with salt and pepper.

Drain the pasta and add to the pan with the salmon. Toss well and serve hot.

# Spaghetti
**with spicy tuna & thyme**

| | |
|---|---|
| 14 | ounces (400 g) tuna steak, cut into small pieces |
| 1/3 | cup (50 g) all-purpose (plain) flour |
| 1/4 | cup (60 ml) extra-virgin olive oil |
| 1 | clove garlic, finely chopped |
| 20 | black olives, pitted and finely chopped |
| 2 | fresh red or green chilies, seeded and finely chopped |
| 1 | tablespoon finely chopped fresh thyme (or parsley) |
| | Salt and freshly ground black pepper |
| 4 | zucchini (courgettes), cut into small cubes |
| 1/2 | cup (125 ml) dry white wine |
| 1 | pound (500 g) spaghetti |

Toss the tuna in the flour, shaking to remove the excess.

Heat the oil in a large frying pan over medium heat. Add the garlic, olives, chilies, and thyme. Sauté until the garlic is pale gold, 2–3 minutes.

Season with salt and pepper. Add the tuna and zucchini. Sauté gently over medium heat until the tuna is cooked through, 5–6 minutes. Drizzle with the wine and let it evaporate.

Meanwhile, cook the pasta in a large pot of salted boiling water until al dente.

Drain the pasta and add to the tuna sauce. Toss well. Sprinkle with the remaining thyme and serve hot.

# Pasta
## with sardines

| | |
|---|---|
| 3 | quarts (3 liters) water |
| 1 | tablespoon coarse sea salt |
| 8 | ounces (250 g) wild fennel |
| 12 | ounces (350 g) small fresh sardines |
| 1/3 | cup (90 ml) extra-virgin olive oil |
| 1 | medium onion, finely chopped |
| 4 | salt-cured anchovy fillets |
| 2 | tablespoons small, seedless white raisins (sultanas) |
| 3 | tablespoons pine nuts |
| 1/4 | cup (45 g) toasted almonds, chopped |
| | Freshly ground black pepper |
| 1/4 | teaspoon saffron, dissolved in 2 tablespoons hot water |
| 1 | pound (500 g) bucatini |
| 1/2 | cup (75 g) fine dry bread crumbs |

Bring the water to a boil in a large saucepan and add the salt and fennel. Simmer for 15 minutes, then drain, reserving the water to cook the pasta.

Squeeze the fennel to remove excess moisture and chop coarsely.

Remove any scales from the sardines and gently pull off their heads (the viscera will come away with the heads). Use kitchen scissors to cut down their bellies and lay them out flat.

Preheat the oven to 425°F (220°C/gas 7).

Heat the oil in a large frying pan. Add the onion and sauté until softened, 3–4 minutes. Add the anchovies, crushing with a fork until they dissolve in the oil.

Add the sardines, raisins, pine nuts, and almonds, and season with salt and pepper. Simmer over medium heat for 10 minutes before adding the fennel and saffron. Stir gently to avoid breaking up the fish. Reduce the heat, cover, and simmer for 10 more minutes.

Bring the fennel-flavored water to a boil, add the pasta, and cook until al dente. Drain and mix carefully with the sardines and sauce.

Transfer to an oiled ovenproof dish and sprinkle the bread crumbs over the top.

Bake for 10 minutes, or until the bread crumbs are browned. Serve hot.

# Spaghetti
# **with clams, chile & arugula**

| | |
|---|---|
| 2 | pounds (1 kg) clams, in shell |
| 1 | pound (500 g) spaghetti |
| 2 | tablespoons extra-virgin olive oil |
| 2 | cloves garlic, finely chopped |
| $1/3$ | cup (90 ml) dry white wine |
| 1 | fresh red chile, seeded and finely chopped |
| | Salt and freshly ground black pepper |
| 4 | ounces (125 g) arugula (rocket) |
| | Parmesan shavings, to serve |

Soak the clams in a large bowl of cold water for at least an hour, changing the water often.

Cook the pasta in a large pot of salted boiling water until al dente.

While the pasta is cooking, heat the oil in a large frying pan over medium-high heat. Add the clams and garlic, and toss well. Add the wine, cover and cook until the clams are open, about 5 minutes. Discard any that have not opened. Add the chile and season with salt.

Drain the pasta and add to the pan with the clams. Add the arugula and stir until it begins to wilt slightly.

Serve hot with the Parmesan and a generous grinding of black pepper.

# Linguine
# **with crab**
# **& lemon**

| | |
|---|---|
| 1 | pound (500 g) linguine |
| 5 | tablespoons extra-virgin olive oil |
| 2 | cloves garlic, finely chopped |
| 1 | fresh red chile, seeded and finely chopped |
| 8 | ounces (250 g) canned crabmeat, drained |
| 1/3 | cup (90 ml) dry white wine |
| | Salt and freshly ground black pepper |
| 3 | tablespoons finely chopped fresh parsley |
| | Finely grated zest of 1 lemon |

Cook the pasta in a large pot of salted boiling water until al dente.

While the pasta is cooking, heat 3 tablespoons of oil in a large frying pan over medium heat. Add the garlic and chile and sauté until the garlic is pale gold, 2-3 minutes. Add the crab meat and wine, season with salt and pepper, and sauté until heated through, 2–3 minutes.

Drain the pasta and add to the pan with the crabmeat. Drizzle with the remaining oil, and sprinkle with the parsley and lemon zest. Toss well and serve hot.

# Spaghetti
# with smoked salmon, arugula & capers

| | |
|---|---|
| 1/2 | cup (125 ml) extra-virgin olive oil |
| 2 | ounces (60 g) fresh white bread crumbs |
| 1 | pound (500 g) spaghetti |
| 2 | cloves garlic, finely chopped |
| 2 | small dried chilies, crumbled |
| | Finely grated zest 1 lemon |
| 4 | tablespoons capers in brine, drained |
| | Handful of fresh arugula (rocket) leaves |
| 8 | ounces (250 g) smoked salmon, flaked |
| 2 | sliced tomatoes, to serve |

Heat 2 tablespoons of the oil in a small frying pan over medium heat. Add the bread crumbs and sauté until golden, 3-5 minutes. Set aside.

Cook the pasta in a large pot of salted boiling water until al dente.

While the pasta is cooking, heat the remaining oil in a small pan over low heat. Add the garlic and chilies. Warm gently to flavor the oil without letting the garlic color.

Drain the pasta and place in a heated serving bowl. Add the lemon zest and capers to the oil and pour over the pasta. Toss well, add the rocket and salmon and toss again. Top with the bread crumbs serve hot with the tomatoes.

# Linguine
# with smoked salmon & horseradish

| | |
|---|---|
| 1 | pound (500 g) linguine |
| 12 | ounces (350 g) smoked salmon, cut into strips |
| | Freshly squeezed juice and zest of 2 lemons |
| 6 | handfuls of watercress, roughly chopped |
| 1/4 | cup (60 ml) horseradish sauce |
| 1/4 | cup (60 ml) crème fraîche |
| | Freshly ground black pepper |

Cook the pasta in a large pot of salted boiling water until al dente.

While the pasta is cooking, combine the salmon, lemon juice and zest, watercress, horseradish sauce, and crème fraîche in a large serving bowl.

Drain the pasta and add to the bowl with the other ingredients. Toss well and season generously with black pepper. Serve hot.

# Chile & prawn
**linguine**

| | |
|---|---|
| 1 | pound (500 g) linguine |
| 14 | ounces (400 g) sugar snap peas, trimmed |
| 1/3 | cup (90 ml) extra-virgin olive oil |
| 4 | large garlic cloves, finely chopped |
| 2 | fresh red chiles, seeded and finely chopped |
| | Salt and freshly ground black pepper |
| 48 | raw jumbo shrimp (king prawns), peeled |
| 24 | cherry tomatoes, halved |
| | Handful of fresh basil leaves |

Cook the pasta in a large pot of salted boiling water until al dente. Add the sugar snap peas for the last minute or so of cooking time.

While the pasta is cooking, combine the oil, garlic, and chilies in a small bowl. Season with salt and pepper.

Heat the oil mixture in a large frying pan over medium heat without letting the garlic color. Add the shrimp and sauté over high heat until they turn pink, about 3 minutes.

Add the tomatoes and sauté until they just start to soften, 2–3 minutes.

Drain the pasta and sugar snaps and add to the pan. Toss well. Add the basil leaves and season with salt and pepper. Serve hot.

# Spaghetti
# **with fish ragù**

- 1 1/2   pounds (750 g) assorted fresh fish, such as hake, sea bass, sea bream, and red snapper, cleaned
- 2   tablespoons fresh rosemary leaves
- 1/2   cup (125 ml) extra-virgin olive oil
- 1   onion, finely chopped
- 1   clove garlic, finely chopped

    Salt and freshly ground black pepper

- 1   pound (500 g) spaghetti

Place the fish in a pot with plenty of water and the rosemary and bring to a boil. Simmer over low heat until tender, 5–10 minutes. Take the fish out, remove the skin and bones, and crumble the cooked meat. Strain the liquid and reserve. Discard the rosemary.

Heat the oil in a large frying pan over medium heat. Add the onion and garlic and sauté until pale gold, 2–3 minutes.

Add the fish meat and 2 cups (500 ml) of the reserved stock. Season with salt and pepper and simmer over low heat until reduced, about 10 minutes.

Cook the pasta in a large pot of salted boiling water until al dente. Toss with the fish ragù and serve hot.

# Spaghetti
# **with baby squid**

1³/₄ pounds (800 g) baby squid

   Salt

¹/₂ cup (125 ml) extra-virgin olive oil

1 onion, finely chopped

3 cloves garlic, finely chopped

1 (14-ounce/400-g) can tomatoes, with juice

¹/₄ teaspoon sugar

1 small dried chile, crumbled

   Water (optional)

1 pound (500 g) spaghetti

4 leaves fresh basil, torn

Sauté the squid in a saucepan in 2 tablespoons of oil and a pinch of salt over high heat for 2 minutes.

Add the remaining oil with the onion and garlic. Sauté until the onion has softened, 3–4 minutes.

Stir in the tomatoes, sugar, and chile. Simmer over low heat until the squid are tender, 20–30 minutes. Add water if the sauce becomes too thick.

Cook the pasta in a large pot of salted boiling water until al dente. Drain and toss with the sauce. Garnish with the basil and serve hot.

# Spaghetti
# **with mussels**

- 3   pounds (1.5 kg) mussels, in shell
- $1/3$   cup (90 ml) dry white wine
- $1/2$   cup (125 ml) extra-virgin olive oil
- 4   cloves garlic, finely chopped
- 1   large bunch fresh parsley, finely chopped

     Salt and freshly ground black pepper

- 1   pound (500 g) spaghetti

Soak the mussels in a large bowl of cold water for 1 hour, changing the water often.

Place the mussels in a large pan with the wine and cook over high heat until they open, 5–10 minutes. Discard any that

do not open. Strain the liquid and set aside.

Leave eight mussels in their shells. Shell the rest and chop the flesh coarsely.

Heat the oil in a frying pan over medium heat. Add the garlic, parsley, and shelled mussels. Season generously with salt and pepper and sauté until the garlic is pale gold, 2–3 minutes.

Remove the mussel mixture and set aside covered with a plate to keep warm. Add the strained liquid from cooking the mussels and bring to a boil.

Meanwhile, cook the pasta in a large pot of salted boiling water until not quite al dente.

Drain and finish cooking in the boiling cooking liquid from the mussels. Add all the mussels, mix well, and serve hot.

# Bucatini
# **with smoked salmon & dill**

1  pound (500 g) bucatini

1¼  cups (300 ml) light (single) cream

3  tablespoons salt-cured capers, rinsed

8  ounces (250 g) smoked salmon, coarsely chopped

1  tablespoon finely chopped fresh dill leaves, + extra dill, to garnish

Cook the bucatini in a large pot of salted boiling water until al dente.

While the pasta is cooking, simmer the cream with the capers in a large frying pan over low heat for 4 minutes. Stir in the smoked salmon and dill and simmer for 2 minutes. Remove from the heat until the pasta is cooked.

Drain the bucatini and add to the pan with the sauce. Toss well. Garnish with the dill leaves and serve hot.

# Linguine
# **with scallops**
# **& lemon**

| | |
|---|---|
| 1 | pound (500 g) linguine |
| 1/3 | cup (90 ml) extra-virgin olive oil |
| 1 | small bunch fresh basil, stems removed |
| | Finely shredded zest and juice of 2 lemons |
| 1 | pound (500 g) scallops, cleaned and patted dry |

Cook the linguine in a large pot of salted boiling water until al dente.

While the pasta is cooking, heat the oil in a large frying pan over low heat. Add the basil and lemon zest and simmer for 2 minutes. Increase the heat to medium-high, add the scallops, and sear for 2 minutes on each side. Add the lemon juice and warm through.

Drain the pasta and add to the pan with the scallops. Toss well and serve hot.

# Spaghetti
# **marinara**

| | |
|---|---|
| 2 | (14-ounce/400-g) cans tomatoes, with juice |
| 1/2 | cup (50 g) pitted (stoned) black olives, coarsely chopped |
| 3 | cloves garlic, finely chopped |
| 12 | ounces (350 g) mixed seafood (mussels, clams, etc.) |
| 1 | pound (500 g) spaghetti |

Combine the tomatoes, olives, and garlic in a medium saucepan over low heat and simmer for 15 minutes.

Add the seafood and simmer over low heat until the seafood is cooked, about 5 minutes.

Meanwhile, cook the spaghetti in a large pot of salted boiling water until al dente.

Drain the pasta and add to the pan with the seafood sauce. Toss well and serve hot.

# Spaghetti
# **with swordfish**
# **& thyme**

| | |
|---|---|
| 1 | pound (500 g) swordfish steak, cut into small pieces |
| 4 | tablespoons all-purpose (plain) flour |
| $1/4$ | cup (60 ml) extra-virgin olive oil |
| 1 | clove garlic, finely chopped |
| 20 | black olives, pitted and finely chopped |
| 1–2 | fresh red or green chiles, seeded and finely chopped |
| 1 | tablespoon finely chopped fresh thyme + extra, to garnish |
| | Salt and freshly ground black pepper |
| 4 | medium zucchini (courgettes), diced |
| $1/2$ | cup (125 ml) dry white wine |
| 1 | pound (500 g) spaghetti |

Toss the swordfish in the flour, shaking to remove excess.

Heat the oil in a large frying pan over medium heat. Add the garlic, olives, chiles, and thyme. Sauté for 2 minutes. Season with salt and pepper.

Add the swordfish and zucchini. Simmer over medium heat until the fish is cooked through, 4–5 minutes. Drizzle with the wine and let it evaporate for 2 minutes.

Meanwhile, cook the pasta in a large pot of salted boiling water until al dente.

Drain the pasta and add to the pan. Toss well. Sprinkle with the extra thyme. Serve hot.

# Spaghetti
# **with garlic, tuna & tomatoes**

| | |
|---|---|
| 1 | pound (500 g) spaghetti |
| 3 | tablespoons extra-virgin olive oil |
| 1 | pound (500 g) cherry tomatoes, halved |
| 3 | cloves garlic, finely chopped |
| $1/2$ | teaspoon sugar |
| 2 | tablespoons fresh oregano leaves |
| | Salt and freshly ground black pepper |
| 1 | (14-ounce/400-g) can tuna, drained and crumbled |

Cook the pasta in a large pot of salted boiling water until al dente.

While the pasta is cooking, heat the oil in a saucepan over medium heat. Sauté the tomatoes, garlic, and sugar until the tomatoes are just soft, about 5 minutes. Stir in oregano and season with salt and pepper.

Drain the pasta and add to the tomato mixture together with the tuna. Toss over low heat until well combined. Serve hot.

p. 278

Pasta with meat sauce makes a complete and healthy meal.

p. 296

p. 298

p. 314

# MEAT

# Meat

**Beef:** Most meat-based pasta sauces are made using lean ground beef, although it is sometimes mixed with pork or sausage meat to add extra flavor and body. Always choose lean beef for a good pasta sauce and for best results simmer over gentle heat for several hours.

**Chorizo:** Spanish chorizo is a type of smoked pork sausage which is usually eaten without being cooked. Mexican chorizo is made from fresh ground pork. If you live in North America, substitute the chorizo in our recipes with a good quality salami.

**Ham:** A wide range of ham is produced in Italy. Top quality ham is made by marinating the pork in a mixture of salt, salt nitrate, sugar, monosodium glutamate, pepper, laurel, juniper berries, and other spices. When produced industrially, this marinating mixture is injected into the ham by machines. The well softened meat is then pressed into molds which give the hams the desired shape. They are then cooked in steam ovens and left to cool in the molds. Curing takes only a few days and the ham is soon ready to be eaten.

**Pancetta:** Is made all over Italy and there are many different types. Made from the belly of the pig, it varies in color from pinky white to dark red in the leaner versions. *Pancetta tesa* is the most common type. It can be made with or without the skin and comes in flat pieces. Pancetta is a basic ingredient in a variety of dishes, and is used to add flavor to many pasta sauces. Bacon is a form of smoked pancetta, that has only recently become common in Italian cuisine.

**Sausages:** Have evolved through the centuries into many different regional varieties. They are almost always made of pork meat and fat, well ground together, flavored with spices, salt, and pepper, then stuffed into natural gut or artificial casings.

**Salami:** Many different types of salami are produced in Italy. Shaped like large sausages, wrapped in real or imitation pig's intestine, almost all are made of pure pork. They take anywhere from 2 and 9 months to mature, and can be distinguished from one another by the way the meat is ground (either fine, medium, or coarse), by the spices and other ingredients used to flavor them (garlic, chile, fennel seeds, wine), and by the different curing methods.

**Prosciutto:** This is *prosciutto crudo* (raw ham) in Italian, so-called because the hams are treated with salt before being dried for 12 months in well ventilated storerooms. The meat is a bright, rosy pink, lightly veined with fat. Prosciutto is made all over Italy, although the best known type—Parma ham—comes from Emilia-Romagna, in northern Italy.

# Spaghetti
# **with meat sauce**

| | |
|---|---|
| 1/4 | cup (60 ml) extra-virgin olive oil |
| 1 | onion, finely chopped |
| 1 | stalk celery, finely chopped |
| 1 | carrot, finely chopped |
| 2 | cloves garlic, finely chopped |
| 1 | sprig fresh rosemary |
| 3 | tablespoons finely chopped fresh parsley |
| 1 1/2 | pounds (750 g) ground (minced) beef |
| | Salt and freshly ground black pepper |
| 1/2 | cup (125 ml) dry red wine |
| 4 | large ripe tomatoes, peeled and coarsely chopped |
| 1–2 | cups (250–500 ml) beef stock (homemade or bouillon cube) |
| 1 | pound (500 g) spaghetti |

Heat the oil in a large frying pan over medium heat. Add the onion, celery, carrot, garlic, rosemary, and 2 tablespoons of parsley and sauté until softened, about 5 minutes.

Add the beef. Season with salt and pepper. Sauté until browned, about 5 minutes.

Pour in the wine and let it evaporate. Stir in the tomatoes and simmer over low heat for at least 2 hours, adding stock as the sauce begins to reduce. Remove the rosemary.

Just before the sauce is ready, cook the spaghetti in a large pot of salted boiling water until al dente.

Drain the pasta and toss with the sauce. Serve hot with the remaining parsley.

# Spaghetti
# **with fried meatballs**

### Sauce

- 1/4 cup (60 ml) extra-virgin olive oil
- 1 small onion, finely chopped
- 1 carrot, finely chopped
- 12 ounces (350 g) stewing beef, such as top round, in a single piece
- 2 pounds (1 kg) tomatoes, peeled and chopped
  Salt

### Meatballs

- 12 ounces (350 g) ground (minced) beef
- 1 large egg
- 2 cups (250 g) freshly grated Parmesan cheese
- 2 cups (125 g) fresh bread crumbs
- 1/4 teaspoon nutmeg
- 1 cup (250 ml) olive oil, for frying
- 1 pound (500 g) spaghetti

Sauce: Heat the oil in a large frying pan over medium heat. Add the onion and carrot and sauté until softened, 3–4 minutes. Add the beef and sauté until browned all over, about 5 minutes. Add the tomatoes and season with salt. Simmer over low heat until the meat is very tender, about 3 hours. Remove the meat. This can be served after the pasta as a second course.

Meatballs: Mix the ground beef, egg, Parmesan, bread crumbs, and nutmeg in a bowl until well blended. Shape into balls the size of marbles.

Heat the frying oil in a large frying pan. Fry the meatballs in batches until golden brown, 5–7 minutes. Drain on paper towels.

Cook the pasta in a large pot of salted boiling water until al dente. Drain and add to the sauce. Add the meatballs and serve hot.

# Spaghetti
# **with pancetta & meat sauce**

| | |
|---|---|
| 1/4 | cup (60 ml) extra-virgin olive oil |
| 2 | tablespoons lard or butter |
| 2 | onions, finely chopped |
| 2 | cups (250 g) diced pancetta |
| 1 | bay leaf |
| 2 | pounds (1 kg) ground (minced) beef |
| 2/3 | cup (150 ml) dry white wine |
| 2/3 | cup (150 ml) beef stock, boiling + more as needed |
| | Leaves from 1 small bunch basil, torn |
| 1 | tablespoon finely chopped fresh parsley |
| | Salt and freshly ground black pepper |
| 1 | pound (500 g) spaghetti |
| 1/2 | cup (60 g) freshly grated aged pecorino cheese |

Heat the oil and lard in a large saucepan over medium-low heat. Add the onions, pancetta, bay leaf, and beef. Cover and simmer for about 30 minutes, stirring often.

Increase the heat and pour in the wine and stock. Add the basil, parsley, salt, and pepper and bring to a boil. Lower the heat and simmer, partially covered, for at least 2 hours. Add more stock if the sauce becomes too thick.

Cook the pasta in a large pot of salted boiling water until al dente.

Drain the pasta and add to the sauce. Toss well. Sprinkle with pecorino and serve hot.

# Spaghetti **with bell peppers & pancetta**

| | |
|---|---|
| 1/4 | cup (60 ml) extra-virgin olive oil |
| 1 | cup (120 g) pancetta |
| 1 | onion, finely chopped |
| 1 | clove garlic, finely chopped |
| 2 | tablespoons finely chopped fresh parsley |
| 6 | basil leaves, torn |
| 2 | red and 2 yellow bell peppers (capsicums), seeded and finely sliced |
| 1 | (14-ounce/400-g) can tomatoes, with juice |
| 1/2 | fresh red chile, chopped |
| 1/2 | teaspoon dried oregano |
| | Salt |
| 2 | tablespoons capers |
| | Handful green olives, pitted and chopped |
| 1 | pound (500 g) spaghetti |
| 1/2 | cup (60 g) freshly grated Parmesan cheese |

Heat the oil in a large frying pan over medium heat. Add the pancetta and sauté until lightly browned, 3–4 minutes. Add the onion, garlic, parsley, basil, and bell peppers. Sauté until the bell peppers and onions are tender, about 10 minutes.

Stir in the tomatoes, chile, and oregano, and season with salt. Mix well, cover, and simmer over low heat until reduced, about 30 minutes. Add the capers and olives.

Cook the pasta in a large pot of salted boiling water until al dente. Drain and add to the pan. Toss well. Sprinkle with the cheese and serve hot.

# Bucatini
## with amatriciana sauce

| | |
|---|---|
| 2 | cups (250 g) pancetta, cut into thin strips |
| 1 | medium onion, finely chopped |
| 2 | pounds (1 kg) ripe tomatoes, peeled and chopped |
| 1 | fresh red chile, seeded and chopped |
| | Salt and freshly ground black pepper |
| 1 | pound (500 g) bucatini |

Sauté the pancetta in a large frying pan over medium heat until lightly browned, about 5 minutes. Add the onion and sauté until softened, 3–4 minutes.

Add the tomatoes and chile. Mix well and season with salt and pepper. Partially cover and simmer over low heat until the tomatoes are well reduced, about 30 minutes.

Cook the pasta in a large pot of salted boiling water until al dente.

Drain the pasta and add to the sauce. Toss well and serve hot.

# Spaghetti
# **with salami**
# **& ricotta**

| | |
|---|---|
| 1/4 | cup (60 ml) extra-virgin olive oil |
| 3 | red onions, finely chopped |
| 2 | carrots, finely chopped |
| 2 | stalks celery, finely chopped |
| 2 | cloves garlic, lightly crushed but whole |
| 1 1/2 | cups (180 g) diced pancetta |
| 2 | pounds (1 kg) stew beef, such as top round, in a single piece |
| 2/3 | cup (150 ml) dry white wine |
| 1/4 | cup (60 ml) tomato paste (concentrate) dissolved in 1/4 cup (60 ml) dry white wine |
| 3 | pounds (1.5 kg) tomatoes, peeled and chopped |
| | Leaves from 1 small bunch fresh basil, torn |
| | Salt and freshly ground black pepper |
| | 1 cup (250 ml) beef stock (homemade or bouillon cube) |
| 1 | (500 g) spaghetti |
| 1 1/2 | cups (180 g) diced salami |
| 1 2/3 | cups (400 g) ricotta cheese |
| 6 | tablespoons freshly grated aged pecorino cheese |

Heat the oil in a heavy-bottomed saucepan over medium heat. Add the onions, carrots, celery, garlic, and pancetta and sauté until softened, 3–4 minutes.

Add the meat and sear all over. Pour in the wine and tomato paste mixture and simmer until it evaporates.

Add the tomatoes and basil and season with salt and pepper. Simmer, partially covered, over low heat until the meat is tender, about 2 hours, adding the stock if the sauce becomes too thick. Remove the meat and slice thinly.

Cook the pasta in a large pot of salted boiling water until al dente.

Drain the pasta and toss in a large bowl with the salami and half the sauce.

Arrange one-third of the pasta in a serving dish, spread with one-third of the ricotta and top with one-third of the beef. Sprinkle with pecorino and top with sauce. Repeat this layering process twice until all the ingredients are in the dish. Serve hot.

# Fried spaghetti
# **parcels**

8    ounces (250 g) spaghettini

1/4    cup (60 g) butter

1/4    cup (60 g) freshly grated pecorino cheese

Sauce

1    cup (150 g) frozen peas

3    tablespoons water + more as needed

1 1/2    tablespoons butter, cut up

1    tablespoon finely chopped onion + 1/2 onion, finely chopped

1/2    teaspoon sugar

    Salt

5    ounces (150 g) ground (minced) beef

3    tablespoons extra-virgin olive oil

1/4    cup (60 ml) dry red wine

1    tablespoon tomato paste (concentrate) dissolved in 1 cup (250 ml) boiling beef stock (homemade or bouillon cube)

1/2    teaspoon dried oregano

    Freshly ground black pepper

2    ounces (60 g) provolone or caciocavallo cheese, cut into small cubes

3    large eggs, lightly beaten

3/4    cup (90 g) fine dry bread crumbs

4    cups (1 liter) olive oil, for frying

Cook the pasta in a large pot of salted boiling water until just barely al dente. Drain and toss with the butter and pecorino until well mixed.

Butter four 3-inch (7-cm) aluminum or soufflé molds. Spoon the pasta to cover the bottom and sides of each mold, leaving the center empty. Set aside the leftover pasta to seal the mold.

Sauce: Place the peas, water, butter, 1 tablespoon of the chopped onion, sugar, and salt in a large frying pan over medium heat. Cover and simmer until the peas are tender, 5–10 minutes, shaking the pan often and adding more water if the mixture begins to stick to the pan.

Heat the oil in a large frying pan over high heat and add the half onion and beef. Sauté until lightly browned, about 5 minutes.

Pour in the wine and let it evaporate. Pour in the boiling stock and tomato paste mixture. Season with salt and pepper, add the oregano, and simmer over low heat for 30 minutes.

Stir in the pea mixture and let cool.

Fill the molds with a little of the meat sauce and the provolone. Top with the remaining pasta, pressing it down firmly. Carefully invert the forms onto a chopping board.

Dip the forms in the beaten egg, then in the bread crumbs, making sure they are well coated. (They can also be refrigerated for 1 day before frying.)

Heat the oil in a large, deep frying pan, preferably cast-iron, over medium heat and fry the forms, turning them once, until crisp and golden brown, 5–7 minutes.

Drain on paper towels. Serve hot.

If you prefer not to eat fried food, sprinkle the prepared molds with grated pecorino cheese and bread crumbs and bake at 400°F (200°C/gas 6) for about 40 minutes, or until golden brown. Turn out of the molds to serve.

# Spicy spaghetti
# **with pancetta**
# **& onion**

| | |
|---|---|
| 1 | pound (500 g) spaghetti |
| 1/4 | cup (60 ml) extra-virgin olive oil |
| 1 | small dried chile, crumbled |
| 2 | cups (250 g) pancetta, coarsely chopped |
| 1 | large white onion, finely chopped |
| 1 | tablespoon finely chopped fresh parsley |
| 1 | cup (125 g) freshly grated pecorino cheese |

Cook the pasta in a large pot of salted boiling water until al dente.

Heat the oil in a medium saucepan over medium heat. Sauté the chile and pancetta until browned, 3–4 minutes. Remove the pancetta and set aside.

In the same saucepan, sauté the onion over medium heat until softened, 3–4 minutes. Return the pancetta to the saucepan and let it flavor the onion.

Drain the pasta and add to the sauce. Season with parsley and pecorino. Toss well and serve hot.

# Spaghetti
# **with pancetta**

| | |
|---|---|
| 1/4 | cup (60 ml) extra-virgin olive oil |
| 1 1/2 | cups (180 g) pancetta, cut into small cubes |
| 1 | large onion, finely chopped |
| 1 1/2 | pounds (750 g) tomatoes, peeled, seeded, and coarsely chopped |
| 1 | small bunch marjoram, finely chopped |
| | Salt and freshly ground black pepper |
| 1 | pound (500 g) spaghetti |
| 1/2 | cup (60 g) freshly grated pecorino cheese |

Heat the oil in a saucepan over medium heat. Add the pancetta and sauté until crisp. Remove and set aside.

Sauté the onion in the oil remaining from the pancetta in the same saucepan until softened, 3–4 minutes.

Add the tomatoes and simmer over medium heat until they reduce, about 25 minutes. Add the pancetta and marjoram. Season with salt and pepper.

Meanwhile, cook the pasta in a large pot of salted boiling water until al dente.

Drain the pasta and transfer to a heated serving dish. Toss with the sauce, sprinkle with the pecorino, and serve hot.

# Baked
# spaghetti
# **with chicken**
# **& spinach**

| | |
|---|---|
| 12 | ounces (350 g) spaghetti |
| 2 | tablespoons extra-virgin olive oil |
| 6 | garlic cloves, smashed |
| 1 | red onion, chopped |
| 4 | boneless skinless chicken breast halves, chopped |
| 2 | (14-ounce/400-g) cans tomatoes, with juice |
| | Fresh basil leaves |
| 1/4 | teaspoon salt |
| 1 | small dried chile, crumbled |
| 1/4 | cup fresh parsley |
| 4 | garlic cloves |
| 1 1/2 | cups (180 g) freshly grated Parmesan cheese |
| 4 | cups fresh spinach |
| 1 | cup (120 g) freshly grated sharp cheddar cheese |

Cook the spaghetti in a large pot of salted boiling water until al dente. Drain and set aside.

Preheat the oven to 400°F (200°C/gas 6).

Heat the oil in large saucepan over medium heat. Add the garlic and onion and sauté until softened, 3–4 minutes. Add the chicken and sauté until browned.

Place the tomatoes, basil, salt, chile, parsley, garlic, and 1 cup (120 g) of Parmesan in a food processor. Pulse until chunky, not smooth. Add to the chicken mixture. Simmer for 15 minutes. Remove from the heat. Stir in the spinach and pasta.

Place the mixture in a baking dish. Sprinkle the cheeses on top. Bake for 25 minutes. Serve hot.

# Spaghetti
# **with Italian sausage sauce**

| | |
|---|---|
| 5 | Italian sausages |
| 2 | tablespoons extra-virgin olive oil |
| 1 | large onion, chopped |
| 2 | cloves garlic, finely chopped |
| 2 | (14-ounce/400-g) cans tomatoes, with juice |
| 1 | pound (500) spaghetti |
| | Salt and freshly ground black pepper |
| | Freshly grated Parmesan cheese, to serve |

Remove the sausage meat from its casings.

Heat the oil in a large frying pan over medium heat. Add the onion and garlic and sauté until softened, 3–4 minutes.

Add the sausage meat and sauté until browned, 5–10 minutes. Add the tomatoes and simmer for 15 minutes. Season with salt and pepper.

Cook the pasta in a large pot of salted boiling water until al dente.

Drain and add to the pan with the sauce. Toss well and serve hot with the Parmesan cheese.

# Spaghetti
# **with stuffed**
# **bell peppers**

| | |
|---|---|
| 6 | medium green bell peppers (capsicums) |
| 1 | large egg, lightly beaten |
| $1/2$ | cup (125 ml) milk |
| $2/3$ | cup soft bread crumbs |
| 1 | onion, chopped |
| 1 | teaspoon salt |
| $1/4$ | teaspoon pepper |
| 1 | tablespoon finely chopped fresh sage |
| 2 | pounds (1 kg) ground (minced) beef |
| 2 | (14-ounce/400-g) cans tomatoes, with juice |
| $1/2$ | teaspoon garlic salt |
| 1 | teaspoon fresh oregano leaves |
| 8 | fresh basil leaves, torn |
| 1 | tablespoon extra-virgin olive oil |
| 1 | pound (500 g) spaghetti |

Cook the bell peppers in salted boiling water for 5 minutes. Drain and let cool slightly. Preheat the oven to 375°F (190°C/gas 5).

Combine the egg, milk, bread crumbs, half the onion, salt, pepper, and sage in a bowl and mix well. Add the beef and mix gently.

Stuff the peppers with meat mixture. Arrange the peppers in a baking dish.

Combine the tomatoes with the remaining onion, salt, oregano, and basil. Pour around the peppers in the baking dish. Bake for 45–60 minutes, until the peppers are tender and the meat is cooked.

Cook the pasta in a large pot of salted boiling water until al dente. Drain and toss with the oil.

Arrange the spaghetti on a serving platter. Top with the peppers and spoon the sauce over the top. Serve hot.

# Spaghetti
# **with butternut & chorizo**

| | |
|---|---|
| 1 | pound (500 g) butternut squash, peeled, seeded, and cut into small cubes |
| 1 | cup (125 g) chorizo (or salami), cut in small cubes |
| | Salt and freshly ground black pepper |
| 2 | tablespoons extra-virgin olive oil |
| 1 | pound (500 g) cherry tomatoes, halved |
| | Handful of sage leaves, coarsely chopped |
| 1 | pound (500 g) spaghetti |
| | Freshly grated Parmesan cheese, to serve (optional) |

Preheat the oven to 450°F (220°C/gas 7).

Place the squash and chorizo in a roasting dish. Season with salt and pepper and drizzle with the oil. Roast for 20 minutes, adding the tomatoes and two-thirds of the sage for the final 5 minutes of baking time.

Cook the pasta in a large pot of salted boiling water until al dente.

Drain well then toss with the roasted ingredients and any cooking juices from the dish.

Serve hot sprinkled with the remaining sage and Parmesan, if using.

# Spaghetti
# **with quick tomato sauce**

| | |
|---|---|
| 1 | pound (500 g) spaghetti |
| 1/3 | cup (90 ml) extra-virgin olive oil |
| 8 | ounces (250 g) diced pancetta |
| 4 | cloves garlic, finely chopped |
| 12 | large ripe tomatoes, peeled and chopped |
| | Salt and freshly ground black pepper |
| 5 | ounces (150 g) caprino (soft fresh goat cheese) |
| | Handful of fresh basil leaves |

Cook the pasta in a large pot of salted boiling water until al dente.

While the pasta is cooking, heat 2 tablespoons of the oil in a large frying pan over medium heat. Add the pancetta and sauté until crisp, about 5 minutes. Add the garlic, tomatoes, and remaining oil. Season with salt and pepper. Heat until just simmering, 2–3 minutes.

Drain the spaghetti and add to the pan, tossing well. Place in individual serving bowls and spoon the cheese over the top. Sprinkle with the basil and serve hot.

# Baked Ziti

| | |
|---|---|
| 1/3 | cup (90 ml) extra-virgin olive oil |
| 8 | ounces (250 g) Italian sausages, peeled and crumbled |
| 1/4 | cup (60 ml) dry white wine |
| 1 | (14-ounce/400-g) can tomatoes, with juice |
| 1 | tablespoon finely chopped fresh basil |
| | Salt and freshly ground black pepper |
| 6 | ounces (180 g) freshly grated pecorino cheese |
| 8 | ounces (250 g) ground (minced) beef |
| 1/2 | cup (75 g) fine dry bread crumbs |
| 1 | tablespoon finely chopped fresh parsley |
| 1 | clove garlic, finely chopped |
| 2 | large eggs |
| 1 | pound (500 g) ziti |
| 4 | ounces (125 g) mozzarella cheese, sliced |

Place 2 tablespoons of oil in a large frying pan over medium heat. Add the sausage meat and sauté until lightly browned, about 5 minutes. Add the wine and sauté until it has evaporated.

Add the tomatoes and basil and season with salt and pepper. Simmer until reduced, about 20 minutes.

Place a quarter of the pecorino in a bowl with the beef, bread crumbs, parsley, garlic, and eggs. Stir until smooth.

Heat the remaining oil in a large frying pan. Shape the meat and bread crumb mixture into balls about the size of marbles.

Fry the meatballs in the oil until crisp and golden brown. Drain on paper towels.

Preheat the oven to 400°F (200°C/gas 6).

Cook the pasta in a large pot of salted boiling water until very al dente (it should be slightly undercooked).

Spread a layer of sauce over the bottom of an ovenproof baking dish. Cover with a layer of pasta and top with meatballs, slices of mozzarella, pecorino, and sauce. Repeat this layering process until al the ingredients are in the dish. Finish with a layer of sauce and pecorino.

Bake until the cheese is browned and the sauce is bubbling, about 20 minutes. Serve hot.

# Baked pasta
# **with eggplant**

| | |
|---|---|
| 1¹/₂ | pounds (750 g) eggplant (aubergine), thinly sliced |
| | Coarse sea salt |
| ³/₄ | cup (100 g) fine dry bread crumbs |
| 1 | cup (250 ml) olive oil, for frying |
| 1 | pound (500 g) bucatini |
| 1 | recipe Bolognese meat Sauce (see page 310) |
| ¹/₂ | teaspoon dried oregano |
| | Leaves from 1 small bunch fresh basil, torn |
| 1¹/₄ | cups (150 g) freshly grated Parmesan |
| | Freshly ground black pepper |
| ¹/₄ | cup (60 g) butter, cut up |

Place the eggplant in a colander and sprinkle with the coarse salt. Let drain for 1 hour.

Preheat the oven to 400°F (200°C/gas 6). Butter a 10-inch (25-cm) baking dish and sprinkle with bread crumbs.

Heat the oil in a large deep frying pan until very hot. Fry the eggplant in small batches over medium heat until tender, 5–7 minutes. Drain on paper towels.

Arrange the eggplant in a single layer on the bottom and sides of the baking dish, letting the edges of overhang.

Cook the pasta in a large pot of salted boiling water until al dente. Drain and transfer to a large bowl. Mix in the meat sauce, oregano, basil, and cheese, and season with pepper.

Spoon the pasta into the dish. Fold over the overhanging eggplant and top with the remaining eggplant. Top with bread crumbs and butter.

Bake for 25–30 minutes, or until golden brown on top. Serve warm.

# Spaghetti & Bolognese meat sauce

| | |
|---|---|
| $^1/_4$ | cup (60 g) butter |
| $^1/_2$ | cup (60 g) pancetta, diced |
| 1 | medium onion, finely chopped |
| 1 | stalk celery, finely chopped |
| 1 | small carrot, finely chopped |
| 8 | ounces (250 g) ground (minced) beef |
| 2 | ounces (60 g) ground (minced) pork |
| 2 | ounces (60 g) Italian pork sausage, crumbled |
| 1 | clove, ground |
| | Dash of cinnamon |
| $^1/_4$ | teaspoon freshly ground black pepper |
| 1 | (14-ounce/400-g) can tomatoes, with juice |
| 1 | cup (250 ml) milk |
| | Salt |
| 1 | pound (500 g) spaghetti |
| $^1/_2$ | cup (60 g) freshly grated Parmesan cheese |

Melt the butter in a large frying pan over medium heat. Add the pancetta, onion, celery, and carrot and sauté until softened, 3–4 minutes.

Add the beef, pork, and sausage and sauté until browned, 5–10 minutes. Add the clove, cinnamon, and pepper. Stir in the tomatoes and simmer over medium heat for 15 minutes. Add the milk and season with salt. Turn the heat down to low and simmer for at least 2 hours, stirring often.

Cook the pasta in a large pan of salted boiling water until al dente.

Drain the pasta and serve hot with the sauce and Parmesan.

# Spinach spaghetti **with false meat sauce**

| | |
|---|---|
| 2 | tablespoons extra-virgin olive oil |
| 2 | tablespoons butter |
| 1 | cup (125 g) pancetta, diced |
| 1 | cup (30 g) parsley, finely chopped |
| 1 | large onion, finely chopped |
| 2 | carrots, finely chopped |
| 2 | stalks celery, finely chopped |
| 2 | cloves garlic, finely chopped |
| 2 | large tomatoes, peeled and chopped |
| | Salt and freshly ground black pepper |
| 1 | pound (500 g) spinach spaghetti |

Heat the oil and butter in a large frying pan over medium heat. Add the pancetta, parsley, onion, carrots, celery, and garlic and sauté until softened, 3–4 minutes.

Add the tomatoes and season with salt and pepper. Simmer over medium-low heat for about 25 minutes.

Cook the pasta in a large pan of salted boiling water until al dente. Serve hot with the sauce.

# Spaghetti
# **with meatballs**

| | |
|---|---|
| 1 | pound (500 g) lean ground (minced) beef |
| 2 | tablespoons finely chopped Italian parsley |
| 1/2 | cup (60 g) salami, finely chopped |
| 1/2 | cup (60 g) grated Parmesan cheese |
| 3 | tablespoons tomato pureé (concentrate) |
| 1 | large egg, beaten |
| 3 | tablespoons butter |
| 1 | onion, finely chopped |
| 2 | teaspoons dried basil |
| 1 | teaspoon dried oregano |
| 1 | (14-ounce/400-g) can tomatoes, with juice |
| 1/2 | cup (125 ml) beef stock (homemade or bouillon cube) |
| 1/2 | cup (125 ml) dry white wine |
| 1 | teaspoon sugar |
| 1 | pound (500 g) spaghetti |

Combine the beef, parsley, salami, Parmesan, and 1 tablespoon tomato pureé in a bowl with the egg. Shape into balls about the size of walnuts.

Melt 2 tablespoons of butter in a large frying pan over medium-low heat. Fry the meatballs until cooked, 10-15 minutes.

Melt the remaining butter in a large frying pan over medium heat. Add the onion, basil, and oregano and sauté until softened, 3–4 minutes. Stir in the tomatoes, remaining tomato pureé, beef stock, wine, and sugar and simmer until reduced, about 30 minutes.

Cook the pasta in a large pot of salted boiling water until al dente. Drain well.

Stir the meatballs into the sauce and heat through. Serve hot with the spaghetti.

# Index

Spaghetti with vodka
& caviar 234

Spaghetti with yogurt
& avocado 44

Spaghetti with zucchini
& pine nuts 158

Spaghetti with zucchini
flowers 148

Spaghetti with zucchini 108

Spaghettini with brandy
& herbs 38

Spaghettini with broccoli
& gorgonzola 132

Spaghettini with garlic,
mint & olives 28

Spaghettini with lemon,
chile & basil 78

Spaghettini with mint pea
pesto 136

Spaghettini with pesto,
tomatoes & goat cheese
80

Spicy spaghetti with garlic
mushrooms 134

Spicy spaghetti with
pancetta & onion 290

Spinach spaghetti with
false meat sauce 312

## W

Whole-wheat spaghetti
with onion sauce 146

Whole-wheat spaghetti
with onion & zucchini 142

Whole-wheat spaghetti
with pear & gorgonzola
182

Whole-wheat spaghetti
with spicy sauce 140

Whole-wheat spaghetti
with cheese & vegetables
120

Whole-wheat spaghetti
with walnuts &
watercress 60